Domenico Quaranta

AFK

Texts on Artists 2011-2016

LINK EDITIONS

Domenico Quaranta
AFK. Texts on Artists 2011-2016

Publisher: LINK Editions, Brescia 2016
www.linkartcenter.eu

Printed and distributed by: Lulu.com
www.lulu.com

ISBN 978-1-326-89292-0

Domenico Quaranta is a contemporary art critic and curator interested in the way art reflects the current technological shift. He is a frequent collaborator with magazines and reviews, including *Flash Art*, *Artpulse*, and *Rhizome*. The author of *Beyond New Media Art* (2013) and *In My Computer* (2011), he contributed to, edited or co-edited a number of books and catalogues including *GameScenes. Art in the Age of Videogames* (2006) and *THE F.A.T. MANUAL* (2013).
Since 2005, he curated and co-curated many exhibitions, including: *Holy Fire. Art of the Digital Age* (2008); *RE:akt!* (2009 - 2010); *Playlist* (2009 - 2010); *Collect the WWWorld* (2011 – 2012); *Unoriginal Genius* (2014).
He lectures internationally and teaches "Interactive Systems" at the Accademia di Carrara. He is the Artistic Director of the Link Art Center.
http://domenicoquaranta.com/

"We do not use the expression IRL," said Peter, "we use AFK."
"IRL?" questioned the judge.
"In Real Life," the prosecutor explained to the judge.
"We do not use that expression," Peter noted. "Everything is in real life. We use AFK—Away From Keyboard."

_ Peter Sunde, during The Pirate Bay Trial

Contents

Away of Keyboard

This book has been conceived as a follow up to *In Your Computer*, the first book published by Link Editions back in 2011. *In Your Computer* played an important role both for me as a writer, and for the newborn Link Art Center as a curatorial think-tank. The idea of bypassing traditional publishing and distribution and embracing self publishing as a tool for creating an editorial series; and the idea of collecting existing content - either unpublished, published online or spread through various publications - instead of commissioning new one, has proven successful, and brought us to publish more than 40 books in five years, that have been bought or downloaded for free thousands of times.

In Your Computer collected essays, interviews, short texts about artists that I wrote between 2005 and 2010 for catalogues or magazines, selected in order to outline my personal journey through net art and media art, from the very first steps to the co-founding of the Link Art Center. It came out of the need to look back in order to take a step forward, to find an underlying order in the chaos, and to separate the wheat from the chaff.

Five years later, I felt the same needs, and this book came about. I looked back to what I've done. In recent years, I've been collaborating more sporadically with magazines. With a few exceptions, most of the critical overviews I've written were published in exhibition catalogues and books still available for distribution, or through Link Editions. Monographic texts about artists, written for exhibition brochures and catalogues, are instead less accessible. Going through them, I realized that they may deserve redistribution, and an higher degree of permanence and stability - which is what Link Editions is about.

The current selection features twelve texts about eleven artists and an artist duo. After closing the selection and choosing the book title, I decided to include, in the form of a second introduction, the essay "Art and the Internet 1994 - 2014. Notes and Comments" that I wrote for the catalogue of the exhibition *Megarave - Metarave*, at Kunsthaus Langenthal in 2014. Someway, for me this text sums up the shift that came along in recent years, and the difference between *In Your Computer* and *AFK*, pretty well.

The artists featured in this book are more or less of my generation - sometimes a little bit older, sometimes a little bit younger. As me, they experienced the impact of digital means of production and dissemination, they experimented with them, they thought about them, and all this is reflected in their work. As Peter Sunde, the co-founder of the Pirate Bay, they think the internet is real, and they spend a lot of time in this real space of life, communication, love, hate, surveillance, sharing, and copying. Most of the works discussed here are made to be experienced in a brick and mortar space, away of keyboard; but reflect the current way of living, communicating, loving, hating, spying, sharing, copying, on and away of keyboard.

Like this book, that has been written mostly on keyboard, but should be better enjoyed away of keyboard; and that, if it's of any value as an editorial project, it's because of its ability to shine a light on our current way to live, communicate, love, hate, spy, share, copy and make art, on and away of keyboard.

_ Domenico Quaranta
Urbino, December 2016

Art and the Internet 1994 - 2014
Notes and Comments

I. Post Internet

> Just as modernism concerned itself with the relationship between craft and the emergent technologies of its era, the most pressing condition underlying contemporary culture may be the omnipresence of the internet [...] this exhibition presents a broad survey of art created with a consciousness of the technological and human networks within which it exists, from conception and production to dissemination and reception. This work, primarily produced by artists living in New York, London, and Berlin, has been controversially defined as "post-internet." [1]

This quote from the press release of the exhibition "Art Post-Internet", curated by Karen Archey and Robin Peckham for the Ullens Center for Contemporary Art (UCCA) in Beijing, says a lot about what internet related art has become in 2014, and how the discussion about it has developed during the last twenty years. The text might best be read by an early enthusiast for net art who perhaps retired to a Tibetan monastery or fell into a cryogenic sleep at the end of the twentieth century and would now like to catch up with the current conversation.
The first thing that such a reader would notice is the authoritative nature of the first sentence. Even the most conservative art critic is unlikely to question this stance today: in 2014, the internet is everywhere, can be accessed by massive numbers of people all over the world, and is affecting everything, from global economics to politics, from cultural production and dissemination to our private and public life. About 3 billion people have

yet to use the internet, but the internet population is growing fast in developing economies, and internet penetration nears saturation in developed countries. Baidu, a Chinese search engine, is today the fifth most visited site, according to the Alexa rank. [2] This may also explain why China is interested in an art "primarily produced by artists living in New York, London, and Berlin", where the world of contemporary art has paid attention to this shift: Nicolas Bourriaud, Claire Bishop, David Joselit, Jennifer Allen, Boris Groys have written pages about it, Hans Ulrich Obrist has organised panels to discuss it, Massimiliano Gioni and Carolyn Christov-Bakargiev have considered it while curating exhibitions. [3] The curatorial team for the "Art Post-Internet" exhibition underlines this change. Archey regularly writes for *Spike*, *Art-Agenda*, *Frieze*, *Art Review*, *Kaleidoscope*, even *Modern Painters*, and organised panels at the ICA, London and Tate Britain; Peckam has also written for *Arforum*, and for two years he ran a gallery in Hong Kong. Nerdy new media art curators have been replaced by contemporary art globetrotters. The second sentence is quite telling, too. When our time traveller left, there was little or no "internet awareness" in contemporary art: there was net art, and there was art that existed as though the internet was not there. Period. Today, an awareness of the internet seems to be so important that it becomes the main focus of the discourse, instead of the use of the internet as a medium.

The term "post-internet" needs some explanation, though. We can agree with most definitions of this controversial term that the internet is not over, of course, [4] but it is now a given for many, and artists interested in it are not forced to do art that "functions only on the net and picks out the net or the 'netmyth' as a theme", [5] but can do physical work and bring this discourse back to the gallery. Although most of the featured artists maintain an online presence, and do internet based works, there are no websites – and, more importantly, no technologies on show: most of the works are physical (objects, prints, installations, sculptures, even paintings) and, to use another label more successful in new media circuits, "post-digital", i.e. rematerialised from the digital. [6]

This is a relatively recent move: since the early 2000s, an increasing number of artists with a focus on desktop-based practices decided, where possible, to leave the technologies at home when they were invited to exhibitions. Software was converted into prints, videos, installations; performative media hacks were documented and presented in set-ups inspired by the ways in which conceptual and performance art manifest themselves in physical space; and the early adopters of the "post-internet" label, [7] whose practice mainly consisted in appropriating and reframing internet content and playing with the defaults of desktop-based tools, naturally looked at video, print and installation as media to operate in physical space.

This was not primarily a market driven process, but the result of an attempt to adapt internet content and processes to the logics of physical space. We should not forget that the first "post internet" exhibition was done in 1997, by the net art collective etoy, when they decided to present the *Digital Hijack* at Ars Electronica as a huge installation of orange tubes and a performance which restaged the way the online performance was orchestrated, instead of presenting its online traces. [8] When net artist and hacktivist Paolo Cirio, the winner of the Golden Nika in 2014 Ars Electronica Prix for the "Interactive Art" category, presents his net-based works as video documentation, printed ephemera and wall printed or projected infographics, he does it not to suit the market, but to adapt his storytelling to the peculiar language of the white cube. [9]

It would not be hard for our time traveller to see that this shift put internet-based art in close proximity to contemporary art. Although most of the artists featured in "Art Post-Internet" have been previously discussed as internet artists, some (Bernadette Corporation, Dara Birnbaum, Seth Price, Hito Steyerl) never were; and we should not ignore the fact that Post-Internet is the first internet related practice to be identified as a trend by the contemporary art world, to be supported by (and sometimes identified with) an international network of commercial galleries, [10] and to be discussed by art fair directors. [11] The war between digital culture and contemporary art has now reached the stage of the trojan horse.

If the post-internet debate helps us to understand how the relationship between internet based practices and the art world evolved along the last twenty years, what about the relationship between internet based art and its main environment, the internet? In what follows, we will briefly consider a few stories that may help us to delineate this change.

II. Hacktivism

At the turn of the millennium, when our time traveller left, the internet was perceived as a battlefield for an army of fighters struggling to keep the level of autonomy they first experienced online in the late nineties rather than an art world for a new avant garde. While the dotcom bubble and the increasing institutionalisation of online public space were mining this sense of freedom, artists with good technical skills, who had grown up on activist mailing lists such as *Nettime*, [12] used their hacking, networking and communication skills to attack companies and institutions, perform fake identities, make online protests, squat websites, spread viruses, violate copyright and privacy laws or simply make some noise. Keywords such as hacktivism (hacking + activism), artivism (art + activism) and media hacking were widely used in media circles. Then social networking came about, rising web giants like Google devised a way to not look evil, and while we were mass-distracted by YouTube videos and fancy MySpace accounts, the web became an increasingly regulated space. Artists started claiming that hacktivism was a performance and didn't need to be effective, apparently forgetting how much they enjoyed it when they were able to bring down government websites, hijack thousands of users, make people believe they were the Vatican or the WTO, and force the CIA to investigate them.

A comparison between *Vote-Auction* (2000) and *Google Will Eat Itself* (2005), by UBERMORGEN (the latter in collaboration with Alessandro Ludovico and Paolo Cirio), is telling. In 2000, a simple html website, some tactical skills and two brave guys were enough to persuade the US political authorities, media outlets as large as CNN, investigation agencies and the public opinion that an immoral European company was selling the votes of American citizens, with the risk of compromising the US presidential elections, for months. [13] In 2005, an effective hack into the Google advertising system could only be delivered after the fact and with a well constructed narrative via press releases and installations, because as soon as Google and the audience became aware if it, it was blocked and rendered ineffective. [14]

Hacktivism in art didn't cease to exist, but mostly became a test ground for imaginary solutions, rarely able to have an impact on the collective imagination. The time when an individual or a small group of people could use the internet as a tool to subvert existing structures was over. The term itself became unfashionable in art circuits, only to resurface, years later, in the subtitle of the documentary *We Are Legion: The Story of the Hacktivists*, by Brian Knappenberger. [15] The movie tells the story of Anonymous, a massive movement of hackers which emerged on image sharing platforms such as 4chan [16] and gradually developed a political consciousness in order to preserve spaces for anonymity and freedom of speech on the internet. Famous for its fight against the church of Scientology and its support of Wikileaks and the Arab Spring, Anonymous effectively refreshes strategies first tested in artistic hacktivism, such as DDOS attacks, cybersquatting, information leaks and massive propaganda. But to do this, you need legions now.

III. Broadcast Yourself

The crisis of artistic hacktivism was related to two parallel processes that unrolled with the rise of social networking: the subsumption – and consequent weakening of the political potential – of the rhetorics of independent tactical media into online sharing platforms, and the development of an increasingly controlled online media space. In the late nineties, the bottom-up, many-to-many structure of the internet, and the increasing availability of personal media such as digital cameras and mobile phones, was perceived as a game-changing development by activists, capable of restructuring the former relationship between media and power. This optimism is well summarised in punk rock musician and activist Jello Biafra's sentence "Don't hate the media, become the media", adopted by the international network Indymedia [17] as one of its slogans. Having a digital camera and an internet connection to hand was seen as a new way to fight against the establishment's control over mass media, put to effective use by street activists during the anti-globalisation movements.

The rise of YouTube and social networking saw the gradual decline of independent media channels, mailing lists and forums. Even for an activist, YouTube is clearly a more powerful tool than Indymedia for the delivery of content to a broader audience; and, as Ethan Zuckerman explained in his famous "cute cat theory" talk in 2008, [18] general content platforms are harder to censor than activist media platforms: you can easily persuade people that you had to shut down a particular Indymedia node because it was delivering dangerous content, but you can't shut down YouTube, because you will cause a wider uprising when people realise that they can no longer publish and view cute cat videos. What happened with Wikileaks [19] proves that Zuckerman was right; but there is a price to pay. In the process of moving from “become the media” to YouTube’s “broadcast yourself”, political agency gets watered down, and finally fades behind waves of selfishness and entertainment; cute cats and camwhores prevail, and everybody becomes the product of the services to which they have subscribed: a bunch of data and a record of attention to be sold for peanuts to an advertising agency that will place its ad over your successful political video. Autonomy has to be pursued within this framework, by interpreting and subtly subverting the stereotypes that the channels force onto you – as female artists like Petra Cortright, Ann Hirsch and Amalia Ulman do in their social media work with the trope of the camwhore; or outside of it, creating your own independent channels or using the few that still allow some degree of anonymity and freedom of expression, such as 4chan.

IV. Life Sharing

But places like this are now the exception rather than the rule. Most of us already went under the Caudin forks of the social web, willingly sharing our personal content with supposed friends – more or less aware of our privacy settings – and inadvertently sharing a huge amount of data that we are not even fully aware of producing – shopping records, surfing traces, etc. – with the companies that provide the service and, through them, with a wide range of advertising companies. Recently, the Digital Advertising Alliance's (DAA) launched a Self-Regulatory Program for Online Behavioral Advertising, [20] that allows people to opt out from online behavioural or interest-based advertising. Testing it, I realised that 76 among the 116 companies that participate in the program customise their ads for my browser. Sharing is no longer an option, and the attempt to protect one's privacy is mostly perceived as a move in a chess game one is destined to lose.

Back in 2000, during the golden age of net art, the Italian duo Eva and Franco Mattes - at the time still mostly known as 0100101110101101.org - started a three year long performance project called *Life Sharing*. Claiming – in what became a masterpiece of subversive affirmation – that "privacy is stupid", they allowed web visitors full access to the content of their computer – included their email traffic – through their website. Later on, in 2002, they added a new layer to the project by manually posting their coordinates to a map on the website through a GPS device. The statement currently available on their website reads:

> "Working with a computer on a daily basis, over the years you will share most of your time, your culture, your relationships, your memories, ideas and future projects. With the passing of time a computer starts resembling its owner's brain. So we felt that sharing our computer was more than sharing a desktop or a book, more than File Sharing, something we called Life Sharing." [21]

The project was discussed as "data nudism" (Matthew Fuller) [22] and "abstract pornography" (Hito Steyerl) because at the time digital cameras were still not widely used, and what was exposed was mainly data. Fourteen years later, we all live in the same glass cage. Mobile devices have to be carefully customised to prevent content being shared on some cloud service, or GPS locations being attached to every picture we post online. Meanwhile, maybe not everybody, but at least Obama, is checking our emails. [23]

V. The Death of the URL

With the massive move to social networking services, the utopian ideal of the web as a frontier to conquer, or a virgin land to colonise, faded out. Setting up a homepage had been like setting up a home place: you had to choose the land, buy it, design it carefully or build it from scratch; whatever you made in the end belonged to you, and was the result of a conscious decision, starting from the domain name. It was on this basis that *Name.Space* – to date, one of the few community attempts to participate in the evolution of the web by proposing new top level domains – started as an artistic project in 1996. Founded by Paul Garrin at a time when "many were spreading misinformation that large numbers of top-level domain names were either unfeasible or could cause harm and "break" the Internet, in order to maintain their market dominance and thwart competition from potential newcomers", [24] *Name.Space* evolved into a company, facilitating some important innovations in internet history.

Websites, of course, still exist, but for new netizens,

setting up your own website is much less common than registering a social networking account. Why do I need a website (and an email) when I have Facebook? If the content management systems popularised by blogging services marked the “ikea-isation” of home pages, an account can be compared to an hotel room, or to an apartment in a gated community. Nothing belongs to you any more – you accept that you live in a place designed by somebody else, with little control over the choice of the furniture and few or no rights to change or customise it; you subscribe – often without reading them – to the service “terms and conditions” and you align your behaviour to them.

Unable to interfere with this new ecology of the web, recent net-based art often comments on it, in an attempt to raise our awareness about this shift in the public environment of the internet. *The Death of the URL* (2013) by Dutch artist Constant Dullaart is a static webpage presented in a 38 characters domain made only of “x” characters. [25] An algorithm makes the website constantly refresh itself, filling up the browser cache – which is the truly dynamic part of the work – to the point of a browser crash. As Louisa Elderton wrote in *Frieze* magazine, “the URL is powerfully presented as a sentimental cipher, suggesting a freer Internet from the past, where software companies were less involved in mediating our search habits.” [26]

VI. AFK

> "We don't use the expression IRL [...] We don't like that expression. We say AFK - Away From Keyboard. We think that the internet is for real." [27]

Against the backdrop of this evolution, a broader shift in the perception of the relationship between the internet and reality, and between mediated and actual reality, has taken place. The internet is no longer perceived as an outer space, the cyberspace imagined in the eighties and nineties as the new frontier that led so many people, in the early days, to add starry backgrounds to their homepages, as Olia Lialina and Dragan Espenschied pointed out in their book *Digital Folklore* [28] and beautifully portrayed in works such as *Some Universe* (2002). [29] As Peter Sunde, one of the funders of The Pirate Bay, noticed, the expression IRL ("in real life", as opposed to online), which emerged on internet chat rooms, became rapidly obsolete as we realised that we spend more time on keyboards (or touch screens) than away from them. Or, in the words of Gene McHugh:

> "What we mean when we say 'Internet' became not a thing in the world to escape into, but rather the world one sought escape from... sigh... It became the place where business was conducted, and bills were paid. It became the place where people tracked you down."

This quote, from the introduction to McHugh's book *Post Internet*, [30] bring us back to our point of departure. It's 2014, and all art is post-internet to some degree. Which doesn't mean, of course, that net based art is over, quite the contrary – because the internet has not ceased to be a public place full of conflicts, and is still to be shaped. This is a mission that cannot be outsourced to companies and institutions.

This text has been commissioned for and first published in *Megarave - Metarave*, exhibition catalogue, Kunsthaus Langenthal / WallRiss Friburg 2014, pp. 37 - 46.

[1] The press release is available on *E-flux*: www.e-flux.com/announcements/art-post-internet/.

[2] For some detailed statistics, check out this presentation, made by the British consulting firm yiibu in April 2014: www.slideshare.net/yiibu/the-emerging-global-web.

[3] A comprehensive list of references would be impossible here; cf. at least: Nicolas Bourriaud, *The Radicant*, Lukas and Sternberg, New York 2009; David Joselit, *After Art*, Princeton University Press 2012; Boris Groys, *Art Power*, The MIT Press, London - Cambridge 2008; Claire Bishop, "Digital Divide. Contemporary Art and New Media", in *Artforum*, September 2012; and Massimiliano Gioni, "The Encyclopedic Palace", in VVAA, *The Encyclopedic Palace. 55th International Art Exhibition: La Biennale di Venezia*, Marsilio, Venice 2013.

[4] Cf. at least Gene McHugh, *Post Internet*, Link Editions, Brescia 2011, p. 5.

[5] Joachim Blank, "What is netart ;-)?", 1996, online at www.irational.org/cern/netart.txt.

[6] Cf. "A Peer-Reviewed Journal About Post-Digital Research", online at www.aprja.net.

[7] The term post-internet was used by Marisa Olson around 2006 in reference to her work and that of her peers. Cf. Michael Connor, "What's Postinternet Got to do with Net Art?", in *Rhizome*, November 1, 2013, online at http://rhizome.org/editorial/2013/nov/1/postinternet/ for an extensive bibliography.

[8] The *Digital Hijack* was a massive online performance in which web users where hijacked from search engines to the etoy website by manipulating search results for specific popular keywords. For more information and references, cf. www.medienkunstnetz.de/works/the-digital-hijack/.

[9] Cf. http://paolocirio.net.

[10] Cf. Brian Droitcour, "Why I Hate Post-Internet Art", in *Culture Two*, March 31, 2014, online at http://culturetwo.wordpress.com/2014/03/31/why-i-hate-post-internet-art/: "The scenes that have been cultivated around Berlin galleries Kraupa-Tuskany and Societe are bad, too. If it's at Higher Pictures gallery in New York I probably won't like it. If it's in a group show curated by Agatha Wara I'm sure I'll hate it. If it's on a cool Tumblr I can't be bothered."

[11] Cf. Andrew M. Goldstein, "Frieze London Co-Director Matthew Slotover on the Rise of the Art Fair", in *Artspace*, October 15, 2013, online at www.artspace.com/magazine/interviews_features/frieze_art_fair_matthew_slotover_interview.

[12] Founded in 1995 by Geert Lovink and Pit Schultz as a space for a new form of critical discourse on and with the net. Nettime is still an active mailing list, and its archives are available online at www.nettime.org.

[13] *Vote Auction* is still documented online at http://vote-auction.net/.

[14] *GWEI (Google Will Eat Itself)* is still documented online at www.gwei.org.

[15] *We Are Legion: The Story of the Hacktivists.* Documentary, director: Brian Knappenberger; US/UK 2012.

[16] 4chan is an online imageboard founded in 2003, originally used for the posting of pictures and discussion of manga and anime; users don't need to register and mostly post anonymously, and contents are not archived. For more info, visit www.4chan.org and http://en.wikipedia.org/wiki/4chan.

[17] Founded in 1999, the Independent Media Center (also known as Indymedia) is a global participatory network of journalists reporting on political and social issues. Cf. www.indymedia.org.

[18] Cf. Ethan Zuckerman, "The Cute Cat Theory Talk at ETech", in *My Heart's In Accra*, March 8, 2008, www.ethanzuckerman.com/blog/2008/03/08/the-cute-cat-theory-talk-at-etech/.

[19] Wikileaks' website was closed in 2008 after a Californian judge's injunction, and in 2010 Mastercard and Paypal froze the organisation's account to boycott donations. For more info, cf. http://en.wikipedia.org/wiki/WikiLeaks.

[20] Cf. www.aboutads.info/choices/.

[21] Cf. http://0100101110101101.org/life-sharing/.

[22] Cf. Matthew Fuller, "Data-Nudism. An interview with 0100101110101101.org about life_sharing", 2000, available online at www.walkerart.org/gallery9/lifesharing/.

[23] "Obama is Checking Your Email" is a popular Tumblr blog and an internet meme launched on June 2013 to mock the Obama administration's involvement in the NSA scandal. For more information, visit http://knowyourmeme.com/memes/people/barack-obama or check out http://obamaischeckingyouremail.tumblr.com/.

[24] Cf. http://namespace.us/about.php.

[25] Cf. http://xxxxxxxxxx.xxxxxxxxxxxxxxxxxxxxxxxxxxxxxxxxxxxxxx.xxx/xxxxx_xxxxx-xx/xxxxxxxxxxxxxxx-xxxxxxx/.

[26] Cf. Louisa Elderton, "Constant Dullaart", in *Frieze*, Issue 159, November - December 2013, online at www.frieze.com/issue/review/constant-dullaart/.

[27] Peter Sunde in *TPB AFK: The Pirate Bay Away from Keyboard*. Documentary, director: Simon Klose, Sweden 2013.

[28] Olia Lialina & Dragan Espenschied (Eds.), *Digital Folklore*, Merz & Solitude, Stuttgart 2009. On this subject, cf. the chapter "A Vernacular Web", pp. 19 - 33, originally published as an online essay in 2005 (and available online at http://art.teleportacia.org/observation/vernacular/).

[29] Cf. http://art.teleportacia.org/exhibition/stellastar/.

[30] In Gene McHugh, *Post Internet*, Link Editions, Brescia 2011, p. 5. The book is a selection of posts published between December 2009 and May 2010 on the blog *Post Internet*, which contributed a lot to initial debates around the label.

Rosa Menkman

2011

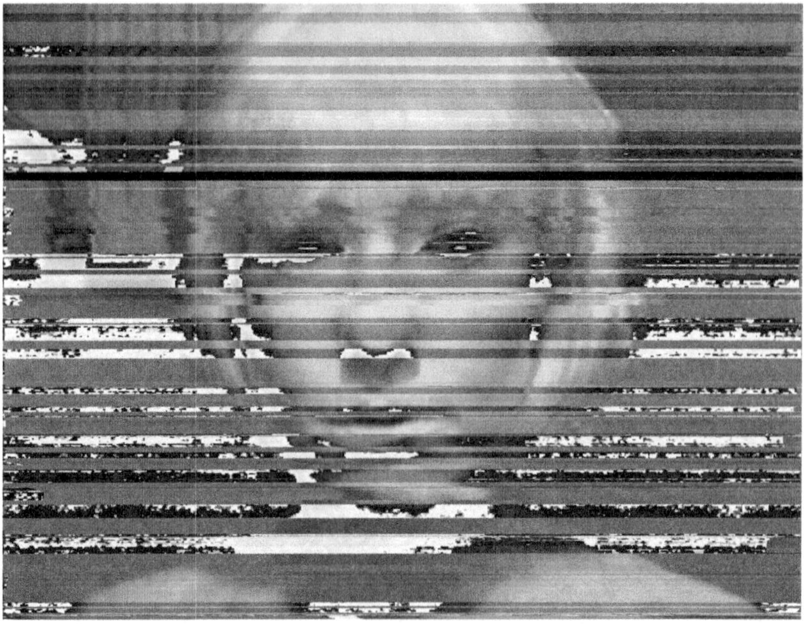

Rosa Menkman, *Vernacular of File Formats* (2010/2011). *Portable Network Graphics (.PNG). interlaced (irreversible databend)*; *Tagged Image File Format (.TIF) ZIP compression, Pixel order per channel, IBM, ZIP Layer compression (irreversible databend)*. Digital prints on dibond. Courtesy the artist

1. Deterioration has always been part of the life of an image. Any image we can think of, from prehistoric cave paintings to the latest Hollywood movie, can be described in terms of its level of deterioration. Deterioration can start straight away or come later; it can be almost invisible, or have a huge impact on the current perception of a given image. In a recent video essay, [1] artist Oliver Laric shows how, paradoxically, iconoclasm made true "icons" of images that would probably have been of little interest for the modern tourist if they were not damaged; and if we think about Romantic painting as dark and contrasted, it is mainly thanks to the widespread use of bituminous colours, that darken over time.
That said, deterioration is usually perceived as negative. The general view is that a damaged piece needs restoration. But what if deterioration is adopted as an artistic strategy, integrated into the creative process? Before the age of mechanical reproduction, Edvard Munch was the only artist to address this. His infamous "hestekur" (a Norwegian term that can be translated into "horse cure") consisted in leaving his paintings in the open, exposed to rain, snow, high and low temperatures, sunlight and humidity, dust and mould, to make them physically "mature" – or die. [2]

2. While deterioration has usually been considered something bad, as a creative stimulus the accident has a long tradition in art: from Leonardo, who looked into the stains on walls, ashes, clouds and mud, to the Surrealists' automatic techniques, the accident – accidental revelations, incidents and mistakes – has often heralded epiphany. Rosa Menkman quotes Paul Virilio:

The accident doesn't equal failure, but instead erects a new significant state, which would otherwise not have been possible to perceive and that can "reveal something absolutely necessary to knowledge". [3]

3. Virilio's interest in accident is strongly related to the zeitgeist of the 20th century. Today, images are not made to last; they deteriorate at an incredible rate. Furthermore, in the age of electronic – and, later, digital media – errors in communication and visualization occur on a daily basis. Transmission goes wrong, storage media get obsolete, file formats disappear, reading softwares are updated. If "to invent the train is to invent derailment" [4] and "to invent the ship is to invent the shipwreck", then to invent film is to invent scratches (as in Nam June Paik's *Zen For Film*, 1964); to invent video is to invent white noise and signal distortions; and to invent files is to invent glitches. [5] Research on technology has been always guided, as Rosa Menkman puts it, by a "dominant, continuing search for a noiseless channel." [6] Artists, on the other side, have always been much more interested in noise, errors, failures, glitches. But why?

4. New media – from photography to computers – are not neutral tools, like a pencil. They have been designed to get a certain result, and they have been perfected in order to make the process smoother and the result better. Let's take photography. Technically, it is a process that consists in "creating still pictures by recording radiation on a radiation-sensitive medium." [7] Yet it has been always viewed as a way to represent reality, and any technical advancement was made with this target in mind.

This is the ideology of the medium. If you use it properly, there is no way to act outside of this ideology. The only way to do it is to hack the medium. Produce noise. Trigger mistakes. Exploit failures.
Of course, a lot of good art has been produced without questioning the ideology of a given medium. Yet, the more that medium becomes a mirror of power, the more noise becomes an interesting artistic strategy. This is why hacking video is more interesting than hacking photography. Furthermore, the more a given medium attempts to turn any creative option into a convention, a filter, an option in a menu – inevitably normalizing it – the more working outside of operating templates becomes interesting. That is why hacking computers – and any computerized medium, including digital photo and video cameras – is definitely more interesting than hacking any pre-digital medium.

5. And that is why exploiting the medium at its best has become a prerogative of mainstream culture, while art prefers, in Nicolas Bourriaud's words, to focus on "the indeterminacy of its source code":

> **[...] today, one must struggle, not – as Greenberg did – for the preservation of an avant-garde that is self sufficient and focused on the specificities of its means, but rather for the indeterminacy of art's source code, its dispersion and dissemination, so that it remains impossible to pin down – in opposition to the hyperformatting that, paradoxically, distinguishes kitsch. [8]**

This quote might seem out of place here. Bourriaud is arguing against medium specificity, and what could be more medium specific than exploiting a medium's shortfalls? This is the dead end that much criticism regarding the current artistic use of technology comes up against. Today, many artists are interested in noise and glitches, low resolution aesthetics, poor images, old media, dirty styles, but also, paradoxically, in an unprofessional, amateurish use of defaults and presets. Is their work formalist, in the sense codified by Greenberg? Definitely not, for two main reasons.

6. It is, first and foremost, a political act of liberation and resistance against control. They focus on the medium because they are combating the medium's "order and progress" ideology – the ideology bringing us to the "hyperformatting that distinguishes kitsch". In order to do so, in Menkman's terms, they

> find catharsis in disintegration, ruptures and cracks; manipulate, bend and break any medium towards the point where it becomes something new; utilize glitches to bring any medium to a critical state of hypertrophy, to (subsequently) criticize its inherent politics. [9]

They do this with the acute awareness that their time is short, because what they are doing will, sooner or later, become a style, a fashion, and a filter in the "tools" bar of some commercial software. This can be seen very well in Rosa Menkman's work, particularly in her crazy jumping from one experiment to the other. She never uses the same glitch twice. She doesn't like effects that are reproducible. She always looks for the unexpected, the unpredictable, the uncanny. She is a true "nomad of noise artifacts". Let's take the *Vernacular of File Formats* (2010), a collection of 7 videos and 10 file formats images where, as she wrote, she actively demystifies the most popular glitch effects. The *Vernacular* is, at the same time, an essay, a tutorial for wannabe glitch artists, and a collection of experiments that should not be repeated, but that will inevitably be repeated until their aesthetic potential is exhausted.

7. Yet, if it was just that, it wouldn't be that interesting. Rosa Menkman's work and, more broadly, Glitch Art and the best contemporary computer-based art is not just an attempt to liberate a medium and its own languages – it is also an attempt to use them to say something that could never be said otherwise. Let's look back to the early examples of the use of deterioration and accidents in art. Edvard Munch "matured" his paintings because conventional painting techniques did not allow him to express the existential drama he wanted to convey. The Surrealists adopted automatic techniques such as frottage and grattage as a means to access the unconscious. The original shooting of the *Vernacular of File Formats* would never have succeeded in saying what its seventeen iterations do say. However interesting as an image, it is the result of a medium under control. It is just a nice, black and white picture file where a heavily made-up Menkman is seen combing her hair (an explicit reference to Marina Abramovic's *Art Must Be Beautiful*, 1975). It is like AnnLee before she was bought and shared by Philippe Parreno and Pierre Huyghe back in 1999: a ghost image waiting to be rescued from an industry that had condemned her to death. Similarly, the flow of data it consists of has been condemned to be always visualized in the same way. In his essay "Art in the

Age of Digitalization", [10] Boris Groys claims that every digital image is a mere copy of an invisible original – the image file. The image file is an invisible string of digital data; the digital image is the way that file is visualized (that is, performed) in a given context. Introducing a glitch between the image file and the digital image, Menkman liberates the latter from its status of copy of an invisible original. The same image is now different every time it is performed. From its birth to its death, it has many possible lives. It is no longer a copy: it is the source of many possible originals.

In the *Vernacular of File Formats*, this story – actually an illustrated theory – is told with an extraordinary level of pathos. The woman portrayed in the picture fades into pixel blocks, gets grainy, duplicates, disappears beyond a coloured camouflage, then reappears, violently slashed. The same oxymoron – an apparently cold, geeky theory expressed in a warm, emotional way - can be found in her video works, especially *Dear Mr Compression* (2009) and *Collapse of PAL* (2010). In the first work, Rosa – impersonating Benjamin's Angel of History – writes a poem to Mr Compression. The dialogue appears to take place in a chat room, and the Angel of History expresses her feelings while a silent Mr Compression turns her attempt at communication into an increasingly corrupted signal. In the latter, the Angel of History reflects on the PAL signal, its termination, and its survival "as a trace" in newer technologies. How poetry can be composed about such a technical issue is something we should ask Lucretius or Raymond Roussel. PAL was the analogue television encoding system used in Europe, South Asia and other countries. Whole generations grew up with it, and got used to its specific characteristics and glitches. And Mr Compression is the personification of a computer process. Do they deserve a poem? According to the Angel of History, they do.

But *Dear Mr Compression* is also the story of a woman talking to a man that makes her suffer; and the live TV performance that originated *Collapse of PAL* was also, according to Menkman, [11] a last attempt to deliver a message to somebody getting the PAL signal. Is this medium specificity? According to the Angel of History, it isn't.

Originally published under the title "Life and Death of an Image", in *Rosa Menkman. Order and Progress*, exhibition brochure, Fabio Paris Art Gallery, Brescia, January 2011.

[1] **Oliver Laric,** *Versions*, 2009 – 2010. Online at www.oliverlaric.com

[2] **Trond Aslaksby,** "The Weathered Paintings of Edvard Munch. Artist's intention, conservation, display – a triangle of conflicts", 1998. Online at www.munch.museum.no/40/6/aslaksby.pdf

[3] **Sylvere Lotringer, Paul Virilio,** *The Accident of Art*, Semiotext(e), New York 2005, p. 63.

[4] **James Der Derian,** "Is the Author Dead? An Interview with Paul Virilio", 1997. Online at http://asrudiancenter.wordpress.com/2008/11/26/interview-with-paul-virilio/.

[5] **"A glitch** is a short-lived fault in a system. It is often used to describe a transient fault that corrects itself, and is therefore difficult to troubleshoot. The term is particularly common in the computing and electronics industries." In *Wikipedia*, http://en.wikipedia.org/wiki/Glitch

[6] **Rosa Menkman,** "Glitch Studies Manifesto", 2009 – 2010. Online at http://rosamenkman.blogspot.com/2010/02/glitch-studiesmanifesto.html

[7] **In** *Wikipedia*, http://en.wikipedia.org/wiki/Photography.

[8] **Nicolas Bourriaud,** *The Radicant*, Sternberg Press, New York 2009, p. 138.

[9] **Rosa Menkman,** "Glitch Studies Manifesto", op. cit.

[10] **Boris Groys,** "From Image to Image File – and Back: Art in the Age of Digitalization", in B. Groys, *Art Power*, The MIT Press, Cambridge – London 2008, p. 84.

[11] **Email** to the author, December 16, 2010.

Jon Rafman

2011

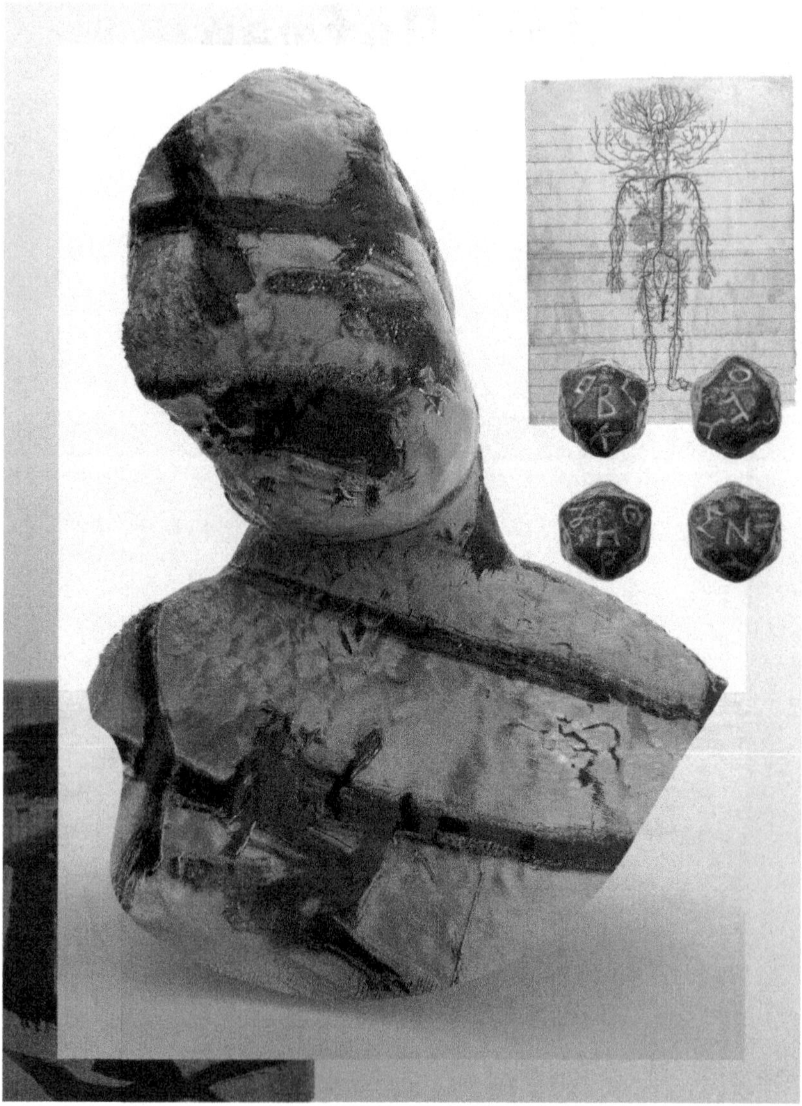

Jon Rafman, *New Age Demanded #1 (Kline)*, (2011). Digital print, courtesy the artist

The age demanded an image
Of its accelerated grimace,
Something for the modern stage,
Not, at any rate, an Attic grace.
_ Ezra Pound [1]

1. On 25 March 2011, the Canadian artist Jon Rafman received a cease and desist letter from Sodrac, a society of artists that represents intellectual property rights. The letter requested an immediate stop to the publication, on the website brandnewpaintjob.com, of images "reproducing artworks, or any substantial part thereof", by artists including Francis Bacon, Jean-Michel Basquiat, Marc Chagall, Alberto Giacometti, Adolph Gottlieb, Jasper Johns, Wassily Kandinsky, Paul Klee, Yves Klein, Franz Kline, Willem De Kooning. On the site in question, for the last few months and at frequent, irregular intervals, Rafman has been creating art works which incorporate images that reference various famous modernist paintings, as well as a small number of contemporary works. He utilizes these images as textures applied to various 3D models taken from Google 3D Warehouse, the online gallery that users of Google Sketchup – a free 3D modelling programme – can avail themselves of to upload and share their works.

This initial communication was followed on 11 April 2011 by another cease and desist letter signed by the Artists Rights Society (ARS) of New York, and its Paris-based sister company ADAGP. According to the letter, ADAGP noted that Rafman had been "displaying and distributing unauthorized reproductions of our members' works, including those of Joan Mirò and Jackson

Pollock, in the context of an online game", and consequently requested payment for reproduction rights.

The work in question is *BNPJ.exe* (2011), created by Jon Rafman in collaboration with his artist friend Tabor Robak, and distributed free online by Extra Extra, a non-profit space based in Philadelphia. [2] Rather than a classic videogame, it is a 3D navigable space that the visitor can move around in, without a precise mission, exploring various settings: indoor and outdoor, claustrophobic corridors and infinite deserts, modernist offices and futuristic cities.

But the distinctive thing about it is that these spaces are entirely papered in textures taken from various ultra famous paintings by artists like Yves Klein, Jackson Pollock and Fernande Léger. The use of bits and pieces of these paintings creates highly atmospheric settings, and it is not always easy to understand the provenance and size of the "loan". Some of them, like the Yves Klein Blue that greets us in the metaphysical, disorienting corridor leading into the world of *BJPJ.exe*, can only be understood in the light of the subsequent loans we encounter. In any case, these artworks are not "cited" in a postmodern fashion, but "deployed" in a purely functional manner: Pollock's drip paintings are well suited to conveying the rough stone of a desert, while Mirò's constellations, teeming with life forms, make a wonderful home for a giant ant, also entirely covered with the same imagery.

2. I have referred to these two recent events, although it might have been advisable to refrain from doing so, to point out the subversive power of an apparently innocuous project like *Brand*

New Paint Job (here on in, *BNPJ*), which actually touches on various unresolved but crucial spheres of modern culture. What makes *BNPJ* a radical project, despite its apparent accessibility, is – on one hand – its not immediate identification as a work of art and – on the other – its referencing of a conception of intellectual property that is not shared by current legislation.
As for the first point, without entering into the legal motivations behind the cease and desist letters, it is interesting to note that neither of them refer to the artistic nature of the project. The first makes a generic mention of "images", and the second refers to an "online game". It has to be said that if Rafman had been recognised as an artist, and his work as art, it is highly likely that it would have satisfied the criteria for fair use: the limited use of copyright material for specific purposes, as normally applies to artistic appropriations. [3] So how was it possible that a collective set up to protect the interests of artists did not recognise, or refused to recognise, the artistic nature of a work? I think the answer lies in the mode of production and distribution of the works gathered under the collective title *BNPJ*. As we have seen, the blog gathers works created by papering amateur 3D design models with textures taken from famous paintings. The resulting images – be they bedrooms or lounges, bars or pieces of furniture, human bodies or classical sculptures, cars or planes, film stars or animals – are ambiguous in nature. Some would not look out of place in an interior design magazine, others appear to be extrapolated from a 3D design tutorial. Their distribution in blog form, but without any kind of explanatory information, does the rest, along with the

title of the project, which lowers the noble pursuit of "painting" to the commercial slang of "paint job". The same could be said about BNPJ.exe, a "software programme" or "videogame": both far from being recognised as legitimate artistic languages.

Even more of a "violation" is the use that Rafman makes of his sources: these are not credited, and used for decorative purposes to embellish a scholastic 3D design exercise. Drawing a moustache on Mona Lisa is no longer a problem. But using Diego Rivera to decorate a living room, Theo Van Doesburg to embellish a plane, or El Lissitzky to jazz up a Cadillac can become one. This is not about bringing high brow and low brow together, but more a question of putting the high into the service of the low, to produce something closer to the latter than the former, and deny the unique, exceptional nature of high culture.

These considerations lead us to the second point, which could be summed up in a famous hacker slogan: information wants to be free. [4] When culture is converted into digital data, there is no longer any way to control it or block its circulation. This splendid axiom, which has been powerfully challenging the survival of traditional copyright for around 20 years now, acquires new meaning on today's net, a sort of huge dump inhabited by barefoot, hungry scavengers who collect, manipulate, reprocess, combine and sell on even the tiniest scrap of information. Nothing, once on the heap, can escape this destiny, not even with the protection of the Artists Rights Society. It is as though the sublime Morris Louis turned out to be the perfect plumage for a penguin badly drawn by a student, it too abandoned on the web. The intrinsic potential of this primordial soup is mas-

sive and, as yet, impossible to quantify. Western culture, taken to the point of exhaustion by post-modernism, is about to be redesigned, not by the web, but by the scavengers that skulk in its gutters, reactivating abandoned scraps, using old tools the wrong way, sticking incompatible things together, remixing code, gulping down anything and then putting it back into circulation with a loud and satisfying burp.
And enabling others to do the same, in a process that is rapid and unstoppable because it is shared in real time by a global community without respect or rules. The age demands... new artists, capable of taking up this challenge, of plunging into this simmering broth and emerging with a new awareness, new languages, new rules. And, behind its pleasing and apparently antiartistic exterior, the ability of Rafman's work to respond to this call is what makes it so radical. Which is why some people find it so threatening.

3. Seen in its progression, through forty or so pieces, from the first *Cy Twombly Lamborghini Gallardo* of 2010 to the recent *Cy Twombly Apartment* of 2011, *BNPJ* looks like an intensive, speeded-up course of appropriation and refinement of a tool. The act itself is a very simple one, the banal addition: model + texture = *BNPJ*. And this allows the artist to work on the details, implications and dialogue between model and texture. Sometimes he uses a fragment of an original work, sometimes the whole thing; sometimes he uses it on its own, at others he puts it with other works by the same artist. The former approach is more frequent with abstract works, which are easier to translate into repeated

patterns. Sometimes he uses other elementary effects of 3D modelling, like the mirror image used in Honda Civic hatchback reflecting a Monet. These choices reflect the dialogue between the two elements: the reflection effect suits Monet, who dedicated his life to painting stretches of water, and Picabia, obsessed with mechanisms, adorns a Monster Truck, while the Oriental-style swirls from a certain period of Van Gogh's do a great job of decorating a Volkswagen Bus, hippy icon par excellence. But as the subjects accumulate, it gets more and more difficult to attribute the end result to a simple operation of addition. The images get more refined, and less outré. Rafman takes painstaking care over simulating the various materials that comprise an interior. *BNPJ* overlaps with other practices, like that – frequent for the artist – of setting his digital images in real space, making it difficult for the observer to distinguish between the end result and a photograph. In the series *Paint FX Sculpture Garden* he maps his textures (appropriated from other paintings or created by him) [5] onto modernist sculptures set in "real" gardens.

We thus come to the series *New Age Demanded* (2011), in which the various stylistic registers and production strategies explored separately in other works come together to form a language of exceptional complexity. The centre of each of these images is occupied by an eerie, mysterious, faceless figure, somewhere between a deformed classical bust and a sci-fi character. The material it is made of changes from work to work – from spiky and iridescent to porous and opaque. The skin comes from paintings by Franz Kline, Gerhard Richter or Robert Ryman, but the loan is almost entirely illegible, fully integrated into the vision. In the background, always in the same position, are elements that simulate painting or collage, or boldly declare their own digital origin. Along with cubes, geometric solids, drawings or prints borrowed from who knows where. The Photoshop levels accumulate, as do the literary, philosophical, artistic and alchemical references. Each piece is a trip through time, between past and future, high art and low art, history and narration. Each piece is a response to what the new age seems to demand of an artist like Jon Rafman.

Originally published with the title "Brand New Paint Job", in *Jon Rafman – Brand New Paint Job*, exhibition brochure, Fabio Paris Art Gallery, Brescia, April 2011.

[1] **Ezra Pound,** *Hugh Selwyn Mauberley*, 1920.

[2] **The work** can be downloaded at http://eexxttrraa.com/bnpj.html.

[3] **For further** information, cfr. *Wikipedia*, http://en.wikipedia.org/wiki/Fair_use.

[4] **The expression** is attributed to Stuart Brand, founder of the *Whole Earth Catalogue*. For further information, cfr. http://en.wikipedia.org/wiki/Information_wants_to_be_free.

[5] **Paint FX** (www.paintfx.biz) is a collaborative project produced with Parker Ito, Micah Schippa, Tabor Robak and John Transue. The five artists anonymously publish a series of digitally created abstract "paintings" on the same web platform, using the most simple, banal default effects of the most popular graphics programmes.

Gazira Babeli

2011

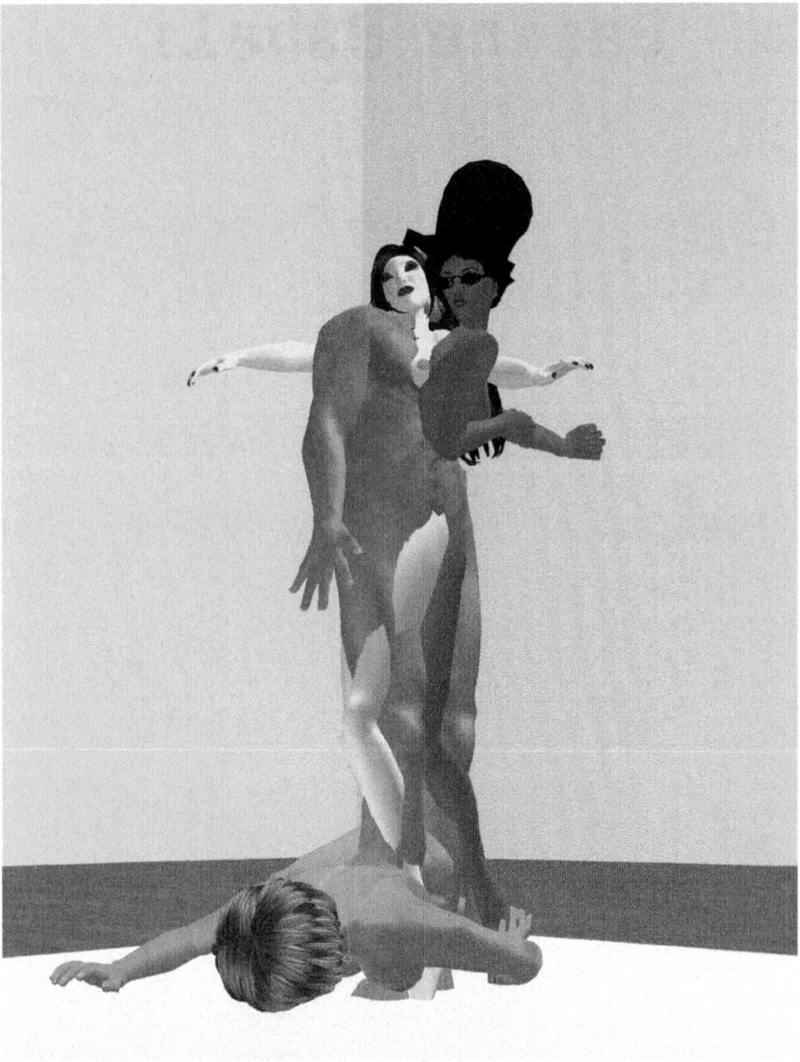

Gazira Babeli, *Come Together*, 2007. Group Sculpture, performance.
Courtesy the artist and DAM Gallery, Berlin.

Gazira Babeli as a whole and Come Together in particular are among most important art project of the last decade.
_ Alexei Shulgin [1]

1. "Gazira Babeli" is the temporary form taken by an artist who has always obstinately stayed in the realm of non visibility, but has managed to forge identities that are accepted and recognised by many as real. The most recent, and, it is to be hoped, not the last – is that of "Gazira Babeli". The name first appeared in spring 2006. It was then that various people sitting in front of computers interacting with a promising new "virtual world" began to associate this moniker with an outlandish character, a tall, thin woman dressed in black from head to toe, wearing a top hat, dark glasses and engaged in dreaming arms in the "workshops" of Second Life (in Gazira's world, as in that of Philip K. Dick, weapons are not designed but dreamt, inspired by who knows what other world, and concocted using code and textures). But the dreamers of arms [2] were not destined to remain the main social group in Second Life for long: settlers, defectors from the real world and the merely curious were arriving in droves, attracted by the siren call of the media and the fantasy of an alternative life.
A hacker among hackers, Gazira Babeli soon began to attract interest from a new quarter: artists. Her unauthorised performances created a stir in a world dominated by wonder, and where wonder is the first sensation to disappear as boredom creeps in. After less than a year, Odyssey, Second Life's first community of artists, that Gazira helped launch, dedicated a retrospective to her which became the first convincing proof

that it was possible to create art inside a second rate 3D software programme. [3] In a world in which artists were falling over themselves to reproduce reality (constructing white cubes and decorating the walls), or sound out the alleged "creative potential" of a software programme designed by someone else, Gazira opened up a third way, based on subverting the users' consensual visual hallucination. You say the word "world" and she unleashes an earthquake or a storm of pop images; you say "body", and she deforms yours; you say "museum" and she fills it with pizzas; you say "Pop" and she traps you inside a tin of Campbell's soup.

If all this was merely played out in the restricted confines of a virtual world, it would have little to say to the outside world. But for Gazira, Second Life is a workshop, a protected space where she could carry out hazardous experiments without lethal consequences. Student of Stanley Milgram and Philip Zimbardo (who in 1971, coordinated the psychology experiment in Stanford prison), Gazira Babeli shut herself away in this simulated reality for four years, subverting its conventions and observing the fall out from her actions. If her world was the Truman Show, and we were Truman, Gazira would be the one dazzling us with floodlights, rewriting the extras' scripts to mind-bending effect and drawing a giant question mark on what we thought was the sky but is actually just a set.

It should therefore come as no surprise that the "outside" world soon began to get accustomed to an artist officially born in 2006, who can be contacted only through an email address or the avatar she deployed in Second Life. This abi-

lity to assert her own reality has always impressed me. Other artists - Eva and Franco Mattes, Cao Fey / China Tracy and many more - have successfully assumed the guise of avatar artists, but in most cases their profile has remained anchored to the previously established identity of their real counterpart. Gazira is the only artist who has managed to lend her mask such an effective reality coefficient that, in the space of a few short months and entirely off her own bat, she has made it into galleries and museums. Even this, however, has its precedents: in the late 90s, "virtual" identities like jodi and etoy, embodied by an internet URL, soon overtook the humans in charge of them; and more in general, the web proved to be an excellent springboard for constructed artistic identities, be they collective or individual: 0100101110101101.org, ®™ark, Mouchette, Netochka Nezvanova, [epidemiC] and UBERMORGEN.COM. Like all of these, "Gazira Babeli" was the first and main work of art by Gazira Babeli.
Between 2006 and 2010 – 24 years in Second Life time, where one day lasts four hours – Gazira Babeli was extraordinarily active, taking part in the work of the international group of performers Second Front and helping run Odyssey. She even bought her own island, Locusolus, as a permanent home for her works. Then, on 26 February 2010, she entered Second Life for the very last time.

2. Given that the software created by Linden Lab is the place where Gazira Babeli was born, and where she took a mainly recognisable form, her disappearance was seen as a "death". The

artist herself played with this story, accompanying authorised biographies with the caption: "active 2006 – 2010". Her departure can be accounted for in various ways. After peaking, Second Life and virtual worlds entered the downward phase of the hype cycle, and media interest, investments and the number of active users dropped off. In a short space of time Second Life lost its unique selling point, which consisted in its being a socially interesting setting: an arena populated by hackers, pioneers, entrepreneurs, creatives, crackpots, criminals and mere window shoppers, where everything that went on received great attention both "in world" and out.

At the same time, art was gradually moving away from "the wilderness outside", and had voluntarily confined itself to limited, protected, institutionalised and incredibly boring settings. When the audience dwindles to a few, annoying, over-enthusiastic latecomers, art becomes a hyper-defined phenomenon and the community spirit falls away, the "scene" dies and the more interesting figures move somewhere else.

But while the game "in world" was getting boring, going "outside" represented a risk. One of the most interesting, and most worrying, biopolitical implications of our current online lives, whatever the system that enables them (from Gmail to Facebook, Second Life to Dropbox) is that we are not the sole, or even the main owners. As a simulated world, in Second Life this is, narratively-speaking, visible. Linden Lab represents a sort of oligarchy of calm but authoritarian feudal overlords, who permit the serfs to work their land en masse, up to the point when they decide to exercise their "ius primae noctis". Which is when you could disco-

ver that nothing you have created actually belongs to you.
In 2010, Gazira Babeli removed herself and her works from the place that appeared to have been the necessary condition of her existence: thousands of lines of code, 3D models, textures, objects created, bought and stolen that made her a living entity and an artist. This gesture can be interpreted, in her words, as a genuine "declaration of independence. Independence from Linden Lab and the internet. A vital act, not an abandonment. A political act, not a question of archiving." Once of the first to experience life in the "cloud", Gazira Babeli is not dead, nor has she fled, but her latest works form an epic escape story.

3. But Gazira Babeli's "executables/standalone simulators" are more than just an act of freedom from Second Life, and a reassuring response to those who feared that the destiny of artists like her was inextricably bound up with a proprietary software and managed by an American company that has and retains the final say on its development, its aesthetic and its contents. They are also a declaration of independence from the art world, enabling her work to circulate not only in the impoverished form made possible by documentation, but also in its native software form: a programme entirely written by the artist using Open Source software, and therefore documented, preservable and archivable.
As Boris Groys observes, [4] the documentation of art, in order to display and preserve it in exhibition venues, has taken off since art started happening elsewhere (or rather, outside of its conventional settings) and in forms that resist commercialisation and museification. This however means that the art world

is now faced with an interesting paradox: the need to elevate to the status of "art" something that by definition is not art, namely its documentation. In order to be commercially viable and museum-friendly, the documentation of art must take on the value that originally resided in the artistic act it documents. Regardless of its usefulness, and the possible good intentions of those who initiated this practice, this stratagem remains a product of a world that is conservative, fetishistic and hooked on obsolete customs and conventions.

Vice versa, software is the expressive language chosen by a series of artists who do not wish to play the game of art according to the reassuring rules imposed on them, but who set out to make the world dance to their own tune. Software as a means for documenting software is the gauntlet that Gazira Babeli throws down to the art world. Gazira Babeli's "simulators" enable her to preserve her work in its original radical form, and not just in its radical concept.

Take *Come Together*, for example. This work came into being in 2007 on occasion of *[Collateral Damage]*, Gazira Babeli's retrospective in Second Life, and consists in a white pedestal that visitors to the exhibition were free to climb onto. Once on this "magic base", their bodies were "possessed" by a piece of software that forced them to perform various dance moves. As other visitors joined in, the work became a unified, animated Baroque sculpture.

The reference to Piero Manzoni's magic bases is more than just linguistic. Gazira Babeli's pedestal has the same function: it turns anyone who climbs onto it into art. But the magic lies in more than just the conceptual shift away from the thought that pedestals call for statues: the software has the added power of making these bodies – perceived as such by anyone who has spent more than ten minutes in a virtual world – do what it wants. It reveals their nature as artefacts, puppets. In a public, participatory context like Second Life, it was logical to interpret this work as "performance art", but in actual fact no-one is performing anything but themselves, their own unique, unrepeatable presence, the fact of existing, in that moment, in avatar form: it is the code, written and executed by Gazira, that is performative. It is the software that is the main ingredient of the magic.

This becomes evident in the "simulator" version of the work, in which the fifteen naked bodies moving on the pedestal are ones that have been chosen and freed by Gazira. Once outside the circumstantial dimension of Second Life, *Come Together* can be seen for what it is: a software artist's contribution to the history of Western sculpture. Behind that glossy, reassuring appearance, Gazira Babeli is a virus in a commercial software programme used by millions of people, a virus that subverts the structures and cracks the surface of the programme. As art should do, it forces us to think about the world we live in, and the new meanings acquired by concepts like identity, body, space, time and society, rejecting the facile truths dished out by those who'd prefer us not to think. As art should do, it takes forms that are anomalous and foreign to the avantgarde academe that has reduced the fruits of artistic labour to an easy recipe for tasteless dishes.

This is why I agree with the declaration of the artist Alexei Shulgin I quoted at the start, and this is why, until she chooses, Gazira is alive and kicking. Long live Gazira!

Originally published with the title "Gazira is dead? Long live Gazira!", in *Gazira Babeli – Come Together*, exhibition brochure, Fabio Paris Art Gallery, Brescia, November 2011.

[1] **Personal** correspondence, 28 October 2011.

[2] **Expression** borrowed from Philip K. Dick, *The Zap Gun*, Pyramid Books, 1967.

[3] *[Collateral Damage]*, ExhibitA, Odyssey, April 16 – June 30, 2007. Curated by Sugar Seville and Beavis Palowakski.

[4] **Boris Groys**, "Art in the Age of Biopolitics: From Artwork to Art Documentation", in *Art Power*, MIT Press, Cambridge, Massachusetts 2008, pp. 53 – 65.

Martin Kohout

2012

Martin Kohout, *Watching Martin Kohout*, 2010 - 2011. Online performance, YouTube Videos. Courtesy the artist.

> At the end of the day I want the audience to touch the surface of the object but without clearly allowing her to do it.
> _ Martin Kohout [1]

When, the 7th of September 2011, I was first asked by Palo Fabuš to write about Martin Kohout's for *Umelec*, I replied with a sound "yes". I know Martin's work since years, I like it a lot, I included it in a couple of screenings, and I already wrote about it. So, I started doing what a zealous art writer usually does: check out his website periodically, go through works, read what's written about them, create a folder on my desktop where to collect images, texts, links and notes.
Then the deadline came, and I didn't have a single line written yet. So, I asked Palo to shift the article to the new issue. He was kind and patient, and the new deadline was so good that I was sure I would have succeeded in doing my job. But it's the 28 of April 2012 now, the new deadline is almost over and I still don't have a single line written. Why? I'm a rather prolific scribbler. I still like Martin's work, probably I love it even more now that I spent so much time with it. I could write pages about any of his works, but I'm still impotent when confronted with his work as a whole.
This is why, at some point today, I started considering this impotence meaningful; not a problem of mine, but something related to the way Martin Kohout's work wants to be approached, understood and misunderstood. And I started writing.
Of course you, my beloved reader, could say: if you can't write, don't write. *Umelec* doesn't need your text to fill up some blank space; and your income won't change substantially if you don't

send anything. Accept your failure, and Palo will be clever and sympathetic enough to do the same.

The reason why I'm going on writing is not, of course, related to my offended ego, neither to my empty wallet. The fact is that, at some point, I started realizing that my personal failure in the attempt of getting a complete portrait of Martin Kohout from the body of his work is just the manifestation of any spectator's failure in the attempt of getting a complete portrait of Martin Kohout from the body of his work; or, if you like, it's just the proof that the artist is succeeding in what is maybe his main concern: bringing to life a body of work that escapes easy categorization, ready-made labels, and the development of a linear narrative; creating artworks that are not the emanation of a strong individuality – the Artist in the Romantic sense of the term – but the result of an obstinate, tenacious, deceptive though extremely coherent, elusive yet honest, confrontation with the world. In this attempt, the artist is not disappearing by means of camouflage – postmodern eclecticism is, itself, a widespread artistic strategy quite easy to detect and to define, and also quite old fashioned and boring by the way; he is literally fading in the background, confusing us not in the way we are confused by a sophisticated collage with hundreds of sources, but in the way we are confused by a blurred photograph. It comes as no surprise that "confusion" is a recurring term in "GIQA Appendix #2", the statement that Martin Kohout wrote along the exhibition *Glare Inland Quiet Attachment* in June 2011, and one of the few statements on his work so far. He writes:

> To be responsible I have to give up Communication – the terror of verbalization and categorization – as the point of departure. I believe there is very little chance to dislocate oneself from the dominant system of Power. The current alternatives don't locate only in opposition [...] so to say don't lie outside of the power structures (as they hardly have any (clear) border) but within them (there is hardly an outside) in "new" (- non-proper) ways of operation across the rigid structures (that being present in our daily practice ever since). The Alternative can be easily overseen as it doesn't appear vividly different. There is no Glare Outland and we have to act in the direct sun. [2]

Martin Kohout is always acting in the direct sun, in a way that makes his work apparently easy to get and define in the first place; but, at some point, we always realize that there is something missing that doesn't allow us to get the final picture. Only after a long time we realize that this missing element is what actually makes the work interesting to us, what makes us wait for the artist to add another piece to the puzzle.

Waterfall

Take, for example, *Waterfall*. What is it exactly? It's, in the first place, a static gif available on Martin's website. There, it's actually the only occurrence providing no contextual information at all: no explanation, no reference to places where it may have been shown, no date. It's just an image, a grainy (why?), round (why?) gif picturing a young male in front of a waterfall, his face covered by a Photoshop filter emulation of the waterfall in the background. Yet, this description isn't completely true. This liquifying effect has been also applied to parts of the body that are left untouched by the water. The face itself is not actually "covered" by the waterfall: it got dematerialized, and it seems to re-appear, mirrored, on the white t-shirt worn by the subject of the picture. These details turn the image into something different from what we may think about it in the first place: an amateur application of a software effect in its "default" form, a practice very common in the community of "internet-aware artists" (for lack of a better term) Kohout often hangs out with.

Waterfall is, therefore, a self-portrait of the artist as he wants to appear through his work: "with relativism, but without ambivalence". [3]

Transparence and opacity

Most of Martin Kohout's works are often accompanied – online or offline – by a short, simple and plain description. Let's take, for example, *The Vehicle-S* (2008): a "series of modified videos of people kick-starting their motorbikes, sound of the engine removed. All taken from YouTube.com and put back as a response to the original footage." Or *No Place* (2009): "Static screening of blue color (lost signal / keying color) on still life with basic 3d forms made from Styrofoam." Or *The Skipping Rope* (2007): "Rotating skipping-rope in the entrance to the exhibition. Easy to jump over from the front side and harder to jump over from the other." Sometimes, the description is even included in the actual piece. It happens, for example, in *OTO* (2012), his latest video piece: "The artist asked the twins to name adjectives describing their mother in a staged recording for two cameras." It's easy to fall into the trap of considering these works as one liners, that don't even require to be fully experienced, since it's

so easy to get them from the description.
When there is no description at all, it usually happens because the piece is somewhat self-explanatory. Let's take, for example, *Moonwalk* (2008), a YouTube video where the YouTube scrollbar and the YouTube loading animation are used as the main elements to design a stair to the sky, that slowly fades into infinity. The video was placed on YouTube, where it scored 386.694 views so far. It was even included in *YouTube Play*, the Google funded exhibition project at the Guggenheim Museum in New York that in 2010 blatantly celebrated YouTube as a pool for "creative video". [4]
So, that's it. Everything is transparent, everything is "acted in the sun". The problems first arise when we go deep into the piece, when we actually start looking closer at them. If we look at *Moonwalk* again, we may realize that what is most fascinating in the video is that the scrollbars are synchronized in a way that makes the red lines proceed all together. Furthermore, when *Moonwalk* was first uploaded on YouTube, the original YouTube scrollbar was synchronized with the ones in the video: deprived of its functional nature, the scrollbar thus became part of the work, even if not part of the video file. This little detail suddenly turns *Moonwalk* into something more than a "creative video" playfully dealing with its frame, or a plain celebration of YouTube as a creative platform. *Moonwalk* becomes a site specific intervention that actually subverts the place of its delivery.
In a similar way, watching *OTO* we suddenly realize that the more fascinating element in the video / performance is actually mis-

sing from the description. Melanie and Tessa Williams, the two twins, don't just "name" the adjectives describing their mother, but they repeat them in a row with a plain, emotionally detached voice, and they look away from the camera when they stop.

Other problems come along when we try to draw a line connecting the works. What do they have in common? They often share similar, cold, impersonal aesthetics; a similar abuse of plain formal or discursive strategies, a similar approach to the exhibition space (be it a gallery or an online space): but more than artworks by the same artist, they look like works by different artists brought together by a curator. Martin Kohout makes interactive environments (*Ombea*, 2006) and online performances or interventions, public stunts and installations, instructional pieces and sculptural objects. This is, again, absolutely "normal", something happening completely "within the current power structures", as Martin puts it: it's the typical approach of a post-medium artist, from the Sixties onward.

But then, Kohout goes back deleting with a rubber the connection line that keeps the works together, and that normal artists – especially young artists willing to define an area and build up an identity for themselves – are more often highlighting with a marker. This is what makes his work opaque and resistant to a second level of analysis. Like Fantômas, Kohout paradoxically enforces his identity by effectively subverting the tools that we usually use to get it. We can take hundreds of shots, but in the end we'll always have a blurred picture.

Site-specificity

One returning element in most of Martin Kohout's works is their site-specificity (or, better, their context-specificity). As an artist familiar with the online environment as well as with the traditional exhibition space, Kohout rarely "translates" his projects literally from one space to the other, but he often addresses the two contexts in similar ways. Let's compare, for example, *Opening Hours* (since 2008) and *The Skipping Rope* (2007). They both address the exhibition place in similar, subversive ways. *Opening Hours* allows us to visit his website (www.martinkohout.com) at certain hours: from Monday to Friday, 7.00 AM – 11 PM; on Saturday and Sunday, 8.00 AM – 12.00 PM. Of course, a website is usually always open. That's what we always expect from the internet: we can access it at any time, and we will always find the same information. Adding "opening hours" to a website doesn't just transfer to it some features of a real exhibition space (the one-liner interpretation of the project): it also disappoints the surfer, in a way that can keep her from visiting it again when the space is "open".

Likewise, *The Skipping Rope* (2007) makes accessing and leaving a usually "public" space an uncomfortable, disappointing, not-for-all experience. How a disabled person is supposed to visit the exhibition? The Skipping Rope subtly subverts the politically-correctness that rules the public space, and introduces an element of "devide" into an analogue space: without the right software and hardware, you can't enter the space.

In a similar way, *Script Pad* (2009 – 2010) is *Moonwalk* translated for an institutional framework. Both the works turn the frame, what's always present but usually goes unnoticed, into the content of the piece: in *Script Pad*, "several art sketchbooks collected by the artist are filled exclusively by drawings based on models depicted on its front pages." But while *Moonwalk* (a digital manipulation of the frame of any YouTube video) can be accessed by everybody, in *Script Pad* the fragile medium of drawing and the context – be it a commercial gallery or an institution – adds another layer: "The work is presented with sketchbooks in various stages of filling from full to almost empty. Viewers are not allowed to touch the work which is presented with an assistance of a handler."

In the same way, Kohout approaches also photographic documentation and editorial material: what's usually meant to document or comment an existing work is often used by him to turn the work into something different. *Robert with the handrail* (2011) is a framed, small picture depicting a friend of the artist, bare to the waist, dealing with one of the sculptures of the series *1A, 1B untitled* (2011), and shown in the same exhibition (*Glare Inland Quiet Attachment* at Exile, Berlin). The picture reminds commercial presentations of products, often featuring a model showing you how to use it. But a sculpture is not meant to be used, and the resulting picture is at the same time banal and absurd. Something similar happens in *Untitled* (2011), a picture featuring a family group portrayed around a weird sculpture that doesn't even exists as an object: a xylophone using YouTube scrollbars in the place of the usual colored wooden bars. Thus, *Untitled* is *Moonwalk* translated into a musical instrument documented into a photo turned into a family portrait, printed on an

A4 sheet of paper and displayed in a standard office file-folder. Similarly, exhibition brochures and catalogues often turn into independent editorial projects. Martin Kohout's interest in publishing finds a recent confirmation in the founding of TLTRPreß (2011), an independent publishing house. *How does a dot come to exist?* (2010) is a single page publication featuring two photos of the styrofoam objects originally used as part of Martin Kohout's piece *No Place*, stacked by gallery assistants before and after the setup. The photos give permanence and relevance to the temporary state of a physical installation in between its public presentations, when the artwork comes with no aura.

Translations

This unconventional approach to mediation should be contextualized in Martin Kohout interest in translation. This interest manifests in many works, more literally in his *Solo Show*, "performed" in Berlin in June 2010. The artist asked a musician to create several songs based on his works. The musician could choose which works and was given total freedom in the composition of the songs: so, the musician is the curator, the interpreter, but also the one who choose the language of translation. Like other participants in the works of Martin Kohout, the musician is given a set of rules, a certain amount of freedom, but no explanation about the motivations behind what she's doing. This makes her an unreliable interpreter, but it also adds complexity to the translation. In *Six Days in Life of Sandra Lolax, Videotaped* (2010), the artist invites a friend (Sandra Lolax) to his studio to help with a project. At the first meeting, she's asked to describe the day only by using

gestures; the process is repeated five more times in the following days. More than a simple process of translation, the performance is a learning system, in which the performer gets more and more aware of what she's doing as it goes on. Something similar happens in the early interactive environment *Ombea* (2006), where the visitor is locked for 8 minutes in a computer controlled environment without knowing the rules of interaction. You stay, and the room is lit and silent; you move, and the room turns into a dark, noisy, scary environment. When you learn the rules, you can play it like a piano, and it turns into a totally different, and maybe less interesting, experience.
In *The Script Involving a Language Teacher* (2010),

> a German language teacher who gives daily intensive German courses is asked to write down the first word or sentence which comes to his mind each morning right after awakening. The teacher should continue doing this for a period of five days without an overall explanation from the artist.

Again, the performer is confronted with a situation in which he's asked to do a simple thing without knowing the reasons behind it. But the second half of the process is even more interesting:

> at the beginning of the following week, the teacher is asked to begin incorporating the recorded words or sentences into his lessons. The words or sentences should be dispersed in the same daily order that they were written down. It is up to the teacher to decide if and how the project is explained to the class and how the words are integrated into the lesson.

I can't resist to compare this performance to what happens when you release a content outside of the safe context where it can be understood according to its intentionality, ie. when you put a work of art in a public space, or on the internet, without the "art" label on it: the signal becomes something different for any receiver, and is further distributed according to these new meanings.

Watching Martin Kohout

At this point, we may be ready to understand *Watching Martin Kohout* as something different from what it looks like at a first look. From April 2010 to March 2011, every time he watched a YouTube video, Kohout captured himself and published it at the YouTube channel called *Watching Martin Kohout*, now containing 821 videos. The title itself invites us to see the project as an attempt to move our interest to what is watched to the watcher, and to the act of watching itself. While many videos got just a few hundred views, some of them reached an amazing number of YouTube users. To round the figure down, we can easily say that Martin Kohout has been watched by at least half a million users. This turned him, with his "distinctive physiognomy" (Gene McHugh) [5] and his weird glasses, into a web celebrity. It would be easy to interpret the project according to the ready made formulas provided by the critical trope of the 'narcissistic video" (Rosalind Krauss) [6] + the vernacular YouTube genre of the "ego shooting" + the performative tradition of the direct confrontation with the artist (recently brought to fame by Marina Abramovic's *The Artist is Present* performance at MoMA) +, again, the critical trope of the playlist as a mean of self-portraiture. But the fact is that we are not really watching Martin

Kohout here. Here, the artist isn't present: he is hidden behind a camera watching at him, and transferring upon him its own features: its position in space, its low resolution, its sensitivity to light. And he is further hidden behind a frame including the YouTube interface features: the scrollbar, the loading animation, the related videos (many of them consisting in video-reactions to the project), the number of views, the likes, the comments. Often, his face doesn't even react to the video, and sometimes the artist is even distracted by things happening outside of the screen – probably on another screen. *Watching Martin Kohout* is a project about absence, failures in translation, site-specificity and manipulation of the audience: which is, to me at the end of this text (itself an example of unfaithful, partially or totally failed translation) what all Martin's Kohout work is about.

Text commissioned in 2012 by the Czech magazine *Umelec*. Unpublished.

[1] Martin Kohout, "GIQA Appendix #2", June 2011. Available online at http://tltr.biz/#giqa_appendix2.

[2] Ivi.

[3] Ivi.

[4] For more information, visit www.guggenheim.org/new-york/interact/participate/youtube-play.

[5] Gene McHugh, in *Post Internet*, July 8th 2010, online at http://122909a.com/?p=2309.

[6] Rosalind Krauss, "Video. The Aesthetics of Narcissism", in *October*, Vol. 1, Spring 1976, pp. 50 – 64.

Maurizio Cattelan

2012

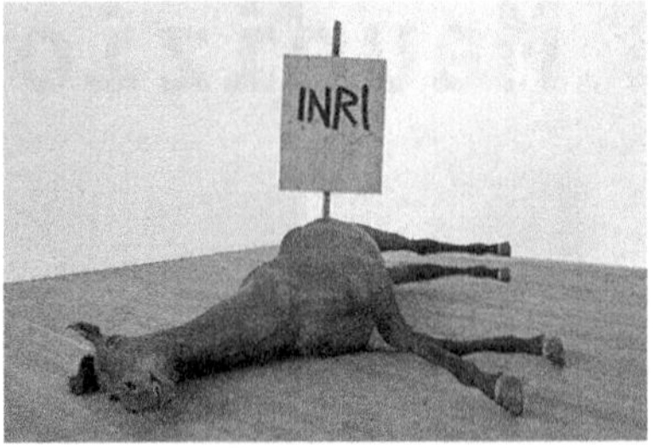

Dead horse (found image, 2007); Maurizio Cattelan, *Untitled*, 2009

The idea is to reorganize something already there, re-present something that already exists. [2]

Open Google.com. Write "dead horse" in the search bar. Select "images". The first search result is the image of a dead horse, lying on tar, a sign knocked in its flank. The sign says: "If you ban hunting, there will be lots of these." The website featuring the image [3] explains that the macabre scene was arranged by some farmers protesting against a fox hunting ban. The blog post dates back to June 10, 2007. The image exists in two versions, almost identical, probably shot by the same camera a few seconds away: the point of view is the same, only the cars on the street and the passers-by change. In the second shot, in the background, a boy takes a picture.

Also, this image has a clone. It was created two years later, by an artist answering to the name of Maurizio Cattelan, in the shape of a sculpture titled, as most of his artworks, *Untitled* (2009). In the official picture, shot by Zeno Zotti and featured in the catalogue of the exhibition "All", Maurizio Cattelan's retrospective at the Guggenheim Museum in New

York [4], the only differences are in the setting – the laminated flooring of a white cube – and in the sign, where the original warning has been replaced by a simple and evocative “INRI”. The framing is exactly the same: the white sign is at the center of the picture, and the position of the photographer brings the beast’s muzzle to the forefront. The horse is reproduced almost literally: the forelegs cross, and the hind legs line up in the very same way.
Once noticed the indisputable effectiveness of the original image, Cattelan made his best to stick to it, and he just took off the incidental details, like the passers-by and the blue rope used to drag the horse in the place where it was found and photographed; and to be sure not to lose this effectiveness as an image, he commissioned an official “media version” of the sculptural work [5].
Yet, these two images are also very different. The first refers to a news item, the latter is a work of art. The first has the richness of reality, the latter the pithiness of an allegory. Furthermore, the horse may belong to a found image, but it has also been for a long time an important part of Cattelan’s iconography, as an alter ego of the artist himself. In the original image, Cattelan sees the potential of a foolish sacrifice, and turns it into a universal icon with a simple but effective reference to the death of the Christ. A minimal shift, but one that turned the found image into something that, indisputably, belongs to Cattelan.

Katarzyna Kozyra, *Pyramid of Animals*, 1993; Maurizio Cattelan, *Love Saves Life*, 1997

Cleptomania

I'm always borrowing pieces – crumbs really – of everyday reality. [6]

Maurizio Cattelan is a self-declared kleptomaniac. In his personal mythology, the trope of the thief comes second only to the one of Oblomov, the idle artist running away from his shows, exhibiting fake medical certificates, inviting people to keep their vote, collecting money to pay a young artist (himself) to avoid working for a whole year, renting his space at the Venice Biennale and organizing another Biennale (actually a holiday) in the Caribbean. Cattelan the thief asked a sketch artist to make portraits of himself according to his friends descriptions; he stole the name plates of some professionals in Forlì; he stole Zorro's Z, Fontana's cut, the Red Brigades' star, the neon sign of a cafe and a pharmacy, an entire exhibition by another artist, and made a portrait of

himself entering a museum from a tunnel dug under the floor; but above all, he stole ideas: from other artists, the mass media, and everyday life.
For obvious reasons, his appropriations from other artists are quite well known. The analogies between his *Love Saves Life* (1997) and Katarzyna Kozyra's *Pyramid of Animals* (1993), both inspired by the four musicians of Bremen tale, have been widely discussed. But the list could go on for long: *All* (2007) makes us think to Luciano Fabro's *Spirato* (1968); *Untitled* (2007), the woman hanging from a door jamb, materializes out from a picture of Francesca Woodman's *Angel Series* (1977 – 1978); and both *La rivoluzione siamo noi* (2000) and *Untitled* (2000) play with Joseph Beuys, his language, his mythology.
Art criticism often reacted to these robberies in an interesting way. Cattelan's detractors used them to prove his lack of originality; his supporters often minimized them, turning them into "quotations" (that would turn him into a late post-modernist, which he isn't). Clearly, the XIX Century myth of originality is still so strong to prevent us to follow an artist where he himself wants to bring us, confessing over and over his inclination to stealing.
What if we choose to follow him along this way, all the way? Let's make a working hypothesis: that theft is Maurizio Cattelan's favorite formal strategy, the one he used the most. That beyond most of his works there is another image, an hidden sub-text, awaiting to come back to light.
This is not an attempt to undermine the reputation that Cattelan's work got along the last twenty years, but to understand

the indisputable success of the images he created; this is not an attempt to reduce his works to the images that inspired him, but to measure the difference between the two; this is not an attempt to demonstrate his lack of originality, but to understand what actually Cattelan's originality is; how he situates himself in the contemporary media arena, and in a cultural environment where, as novelist Cory Doctorow said, "we copy like we breath"; [7] and what he has in common with a new generation of artists for which appropriation is no more a subversive cultural strategy coming with an ideological baggage, but a natural, daily gesture, an habit, a way to contribute to an ongoing discourse. [8]

Permanent Food

> Spector. "What constitutes a successful work for you?"
> Cattelan. "I like when the work becomes an image". [9]

Maurizio Cattelan has an absolute respect for images. The confirmation comes from the quote above, where the word "image" is used with a strong, unusual meaning, in some ways closer to the medieval concept of "icon", or the modern concept of "meme". In this sense, an "image" is a visual sign that circulates outside of the context in which it was produced; something which imprints itself into one's memory, and which is reused, duplicated, altered by anybody, losing all ties with its "author" and developing new meanings any time it is used. It is something that doesn't exist as a "work", but as a "subject" with its own life, able to self-replicate and to spread itself.

Just a few artists are able to create "images" of this kind. With rare exceptions, the visual imagery produced by contemporary art remains within its jurisdiction. For the most part, the collective imagery of the twentieth century has been developed, rather than by artists, by other professional image-makers: film directors, photographers, cartoonists, designers, illustrators.
In this context, Maurizio Cattelan stands out as an exception. The Italian artist, who made such a few "artworks" along his short career, circulated much more "images" than any other artist of his time. How did it happen?
My answer is: feeding on images. An act of feeding that isn't just stealing, but that rather improves an image which, once it's out there, should be considered a commons, no more a property. Filtering, like a sieve, the tons of images that the media – newspapers, magazines, TV, the internet – pump on him (and on anybody else), and choosing the ones that he like and that better fit in his agenda, Cattelan rephrases them and sets them free in the communication flow again, allowing other people to find a new meaning for them.
This is, you may say, what any artist does, but what makes Cattelan unique is his hunger, his instinct, his ability to synthesize, his methodology and determination in producing artworks able to become an image, to enter the collective imagery and be reproduced and distributed in any kind of communication system. As Francesco Bonami said: "Cattelan's works have three lives. They live in reality, in the media and in memory. Their first life is human, the second is spiritual, the third is eternal." [10]

Mike the Headless Chicken; Picture from *Toilet Paper*, November 2011

This reference to the semantic field of food is not accidental, since Cattelan himself (and his spokespersons) used it many times. Massimiliano Gioni recently referred to him as a "great consumer of images", and talked about his "bulimia of images". [11] Back in 1996, together with Dominique Gonzalez-Foerster and the designer Paola Manfrin, Cattelan conceived a magazine called *Permanent Food*, published in 15 issues up to 2007. *Permanent Food* describes itself as a "second generation magazine", declares a "free copyright" and samples images from any kind of source: fashion magazines, illustrations, posters, art magazines, newspapers, fanzines, catalogues, and, of course, the internet. Everything is presented out of its context, without text labels and references, cleaned out from its functional status of advertisement, work of art, amateurish creation, and from its own history. *Permanent Food* is literally what the title declares: a permanent act of feeding imagination, thanks to what's selected and to the way it was put together – an ephemeral assemblage open to the contribution of the user, since the binding

has a tendency to break up. In other words, the magazine is an ode to re-use, a collage meant to be destroyed and put together again, a work of appropriation and sharing.
The semantic area of food is recalled also in the scatological title of *Toilet Paper*, Cattelan's brand new magazine, launched with the fashion photographer Pierpaolo Ferrari in 2010, after his farewell to art. It is, again, a magazine made only with images, but these images are not stolen, but original, professionally produced in a studio. As Pierpaolo Ferrari explained:

> **Every image is the result of an idea, often simple, and later becomes a complex orchestration of people participating in a tableaux vivant. This project is also a relief valve for our minds. We both work in fields where thousands of images circulate. Producing images is part of our job... [12]**

And yet theft, sometimes announced, more often not, takes place in *Toilet Paper* as well. Let's take, for example, the November 2011 issue. The back cover declares its inspirations: Mike the Headless Chicken, Mario Sorrenti, Richard Avedon. Mike the Headless Chicken was a chicken that lived for 18 months after his head had been mostly cut off. The story dates back to the Forties, and was largely discussed in the media. The image published in *Toilet Paper* is a faithful reproduction of one of Mike's best known photographic portraits: the chicken stands firmly, its head on the table, right in front of its legs.
Mario Sorrenti, an Italian fashion photographer, inspired the image of an anonymous model in pants, her body covered by an horde of yellow clothes pegs. As in the case of the dead horse, the differences between the copy and the original are minimal:

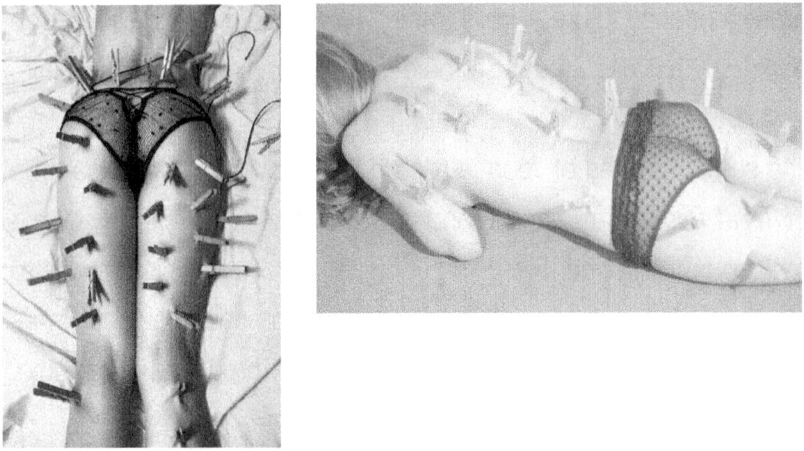

Mario Sorrenti; picture from *Toilet Paper*, November 2011

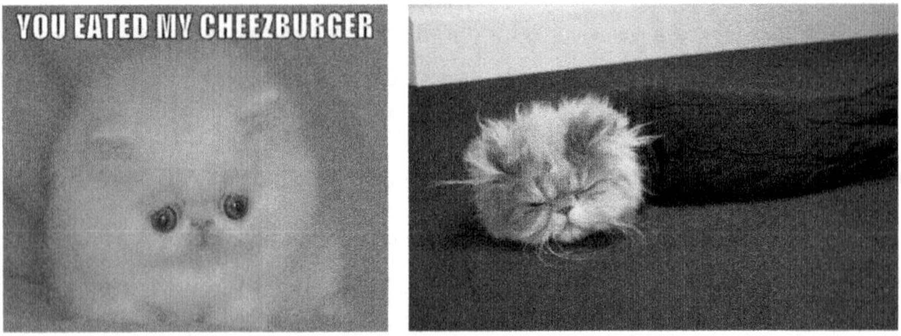

A LOLcat; picture from *Toilet Paper*, November 2011

Sorrenti's black and white photo became a color photography, the layout changed from vertical to landscape. When the original image works well, variations are, for Cattelan, useless mannerisms: much better to keep it as it is.

It's not easy to say how many other thefts, or loans, can be found in the various issues of *Toilet Paper*. Here, like in *Permanent Food*, Cattelan explores the underworld, choosing images cultivated in small niches, with a low level of visibility and not, like a pop artist, images that already entered mainstream culture. However, it's quite easy to find, in the issue we are considering, the tribute paid to the cute cat meme. Well rooted in the popular imagery, this interest for cute cat pictures literally exploded online, where they have been shared and modified, adding short notes in a grammatically incorrect English that turned them into "LOLcats" [13]. Without any text, *Toilet Paper*'s cute cat photo seems to be there waiting for its own transformation into an "image".

Internet Memes

> If you have an apple and I have an apple and we exchange these apples then you and I will still each have one apple. But if you have an idea and I have an idea and we exchange these ideas, then each of us will have two ideas. _ George Bernard Shaw [14]

The last example brings us back to the internet: a context that, according to what I wrote so far, is interesting for at least three reasons. First the internet, however ephemeral and always changing, offers good opportunities to keep track of the life of an image. Even when the original gets lost, images are often copied and uploaded to other websites. Often they are tagged in ways that make it possible to get them back from the nowhere where they disappeared thanks to a simple "Google Search". In other words, while it might be difficult or even impossible to trace the origin of an image seen on a magazine, an underground fanzine or a wall, online it's relatively easier to find what Cattelan saw, years ago, and inspired him a new work. There, the reach of his plumb can still be measured.

Internet found image, undated; Maurizio Cattelan, *Untitled*, 2002

Second, the internet is an extraordinary place for the circulation of images. An horizontal, democratic, bottom-up medium, the internet allows an image to become successful without making its appearance on the mass media in the first place. Internet images don't belong to anybody, they are public domain. They spread and are used and abused according to their own potential, and not thanks to the firepower of those who make and distribute them. There, you don't need money, powerful means of production and authority to be seen by millions of people: you just have to satisfy a specific need at a specific time, according to rules that's not easy to convert into a recipe. Did you ever make eye contact with the dramatic chipmunk? Did you ever dance listening to Charlie Schmidt's keyboard cat? Did you ever share a lolcat on Facebook? If you are able to use it, the internet is an extraordinary source of "images", and an addiction for those who are, like Cattelan, hungry of them.

Last but not least, the internet is the place where the idea of copyright that Cattelan adopted in his work as an artist and as an editor was actually developed in the first place. George

Bernard Shaw's sentence, quoted at the beginning of this paragraph, was displayed full page in the 11th issue of *Permanent Food*. That sentence is probably one of the most sampled quotes of the digital age, first appropriated by the free software community, and later by those who would like to apply the same model to any kind of cultural artifact.

Besides the dead horse, there are at least two more works by Maurizio Cattelan whose origin can be found for sure in an internet image. The first is a 2002 sculpture, as well called *Untitled* (2002), displaying a taxidermied donkey suspended to an overloaded cart. Cattelan found inspiration in an image widely circulated online in the late Nineties, shot somewhere in the Middle East and still quite easy to find googling "funny donkey". This appropriation – mentioned also on the Guggenheim catalogue – strikes, again, for its transparency: in the official, "media version" of the work, now part of the Dakis Joannou collection – the framing is the same of the original image, and the visitor walking on the left is in the same position, and plays the same role in the economy of the image, of the Arab man watching the bizarre incident.

The third work, *Untitled* (2009), is a sculpture in polyurethane rubber and steel of a black rubber boot stretched over the bust of a human head. The original picture dates back to 2006, and was largely circulated around the Web, probably thanks to its fetishist and masochist implication, as a fast Google search for "rubber boot head" immediately shows. Cattelan reconstructs the vernacular image, playing with its high culture associations (Fantomas, Surrealist objects) and finding for it a position in his

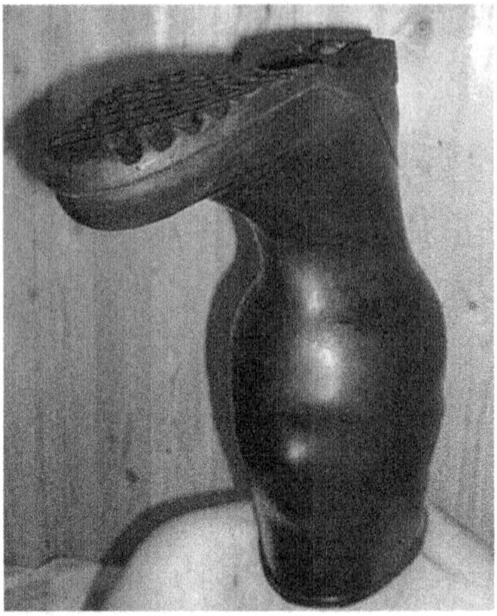

"Rubber book head" meme, ante 2006; Maurizio Cattelan, *Untitled*, 2009.
Below: demotivational posters

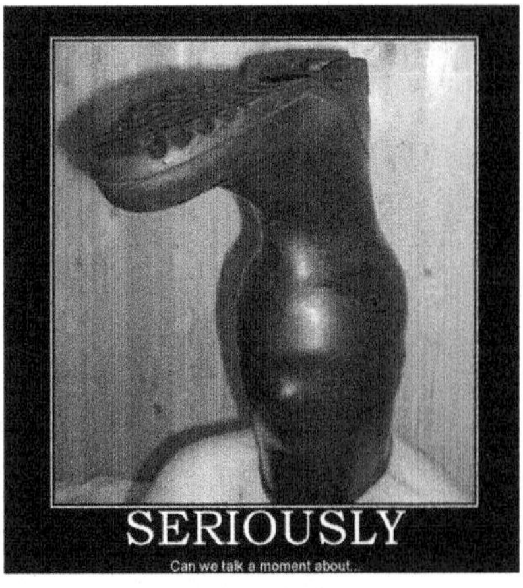

long gallery of self-portraits. Again, the official picture (shot by Zeno Zotti) displays the same framing of the original meme.
In this case, "meme" is the right word, because the image has been appropriated and used as well by many other anonymous web users. A comparison between Cattelan's work and these vernacular appropriation of the same image is interesting. Whatever the purpose that originated the image was, the picture of the rubber boot head was used in many "demotivationals", images created using a standard layout (a black frame with a sarcastic text label) that makes the picture "say" different things any time: jokes about originality, the right use of rubber boots, the safety of using it that way, or... diarrhea. Using a different language and approaching different audiences, Cattelan and the other users who appropriated the same image are actually doing the same thing: using an image produced by others to say something that belongs to them.
True, a swallow doesn't make a summer. But three, demonstrable references do not only support the main idea developed in this essay – that theft is one of Cattelan's favorite artistic strategies – but also its main corollary – that the internet is one of his favorite sources, and one of the archives we have to browse if we want to trace the origins of his images. They invite us to focus on works whose dependance on existing images has still to be proved. They provide a fertile ground for research and hypotheses. In many cases, of course, it will be almost impossible to prove these hypotheses without a complete access to Cattelan's "browser", his physical, or mental, archive of images. An archive that promises to be huge, because of his hunger of

Stupid Horse (found internet images); Maurizio Cattelan, *Untitled*, 2007.
Below: Anonymous online image, 2007; Maurizio Cattelan, *Untitled*, 2008

images and because his familiarity with the internet started very early. Back in 1996, the American website Ada'web launched, in collaboration with *Permanent Food*, *Permanent Foam*, "a second generation webzine with a selection of pages taken from sites all over the world wide web." The website – an ancestor of Delicious, allowing user to visit a collection of links and to contribute with his own links – is now a collection of "404 not found" pages, but it allows us to date Cattelan's interest in the World Wide Web [15].

A work whose "internet pedigree" is likely, but difficult to prove is *Untitled* (2007), the sculpture of a suspended horse with its head stuck in the wall. Look for "stupid horse" on Google Images and you will immediately see the similarity with the image of an horse with the head stuck in a tree. In this case, some changes have been made: Cattelan's horse is not sitting on the floor, but suspended at a considerable height, as if it got caught in the wall while jumping an obstacle, or as if it is the back side of an invisible hunting trophy mounted on the other side of the wall; and still, the similarities with the found image are quite strong.

The same ambiguity can be found in *Untitled* (2008), a sculpture featuring two abandoned shoes with plants growing in them. Apparently, this work was inspired by an image posted in 2007 on an Iraqi blog called "Soldier at home". The two images display the same kind of shoes, and the same kind of plants; the framing is different, but they are both set on a threshold. Cattelan's sculpture was made for an exhibition in a Nineteenth-century former synagogue in Germany, that survived the Nazis because a farmer employed it as a barn. But if its relationship

Found online images; Maurizio Cattelan, *A Perfect Day*, 1999

with the Iraqi blog's image could be proved, we'd probably understand more about the peaceful sadness, and the sense of impermanence that it generates in the viewer. Again, Cattelan appropriates a found image, giving it a new meaning and reintroducing it in the media landscape, allowing others to use it as well.

Yet, the relationship between these two images is mined by the emergence of many other, similar images. Using shoes as flowerpots seems to be quite a popular activity, as proven by searching for "shoes planters" on Google. So, the question is: is *Untitled* (2008) a classical example of appropriation, or rather part of the ongoing history of a meme?

The fact is that Cattelan's work establishes a give-and-take relationship with the vernacular imagery circulating on the internet; and this relationship is extremely suggestive, even when it isn't fully demonstrable. A tentative phenomenology of this relationship could be articulated like this:

1. Direct appropriation: Cattelan sees an image, and turns it into something else.
2. Preliminary research: Cattelan wants to do something, and before doing it he starts a web search for related keywords, in order to study similar visual solutions and finally come up with a successful image.
3. Interference: Cattelan's image is part of an ongoing flow, or, as we said before, of the ongoing history of a meme.

Most of the examples we provided so far probably belong to either the first or the second category: Cattelan finds the image of the dead horse and decides to turn it into a work of art; or he wants to write a new story for his favorite alter ego, starts a web search for "stupid horse", finds an image and use it as a starting point for a new work. But what about, for example, *A Perfect Day* (1999), where he taped to the wall his gallerist Massimo de Carlo? Is it just another occurrence of the "taped to the wall meme", that produced a plethora of pics and YouTube videos easily available online, or the starting point for it? Did Cattelan appropriate an image, contribute to a meme or start it?
And again: what is the relationship between *Untitled* (2000), a picture of a man with a big cork in his mouth, and the pictures of freaks filling their mouth with almost everything? Or between *Betsy* (2002), the old lady sitting in the fridge, and the dozens of pretty girls who tried to do the same? May the two bunnies with

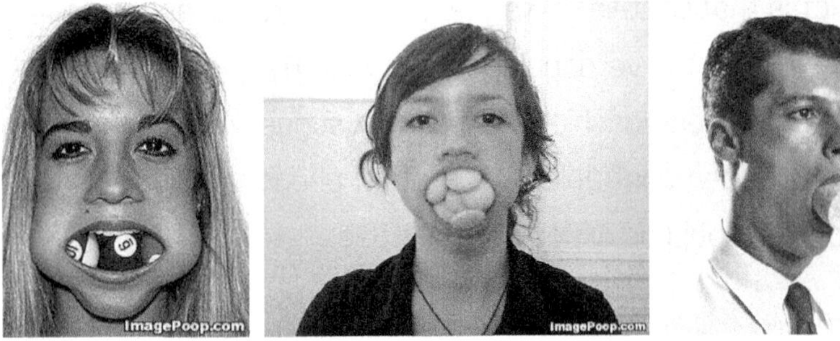

Found internet images; Maurizio Cattelan, *Untitled*, 2000.
Below: Found internet images; Maurizio Cattelan, *Untitled*, 1996

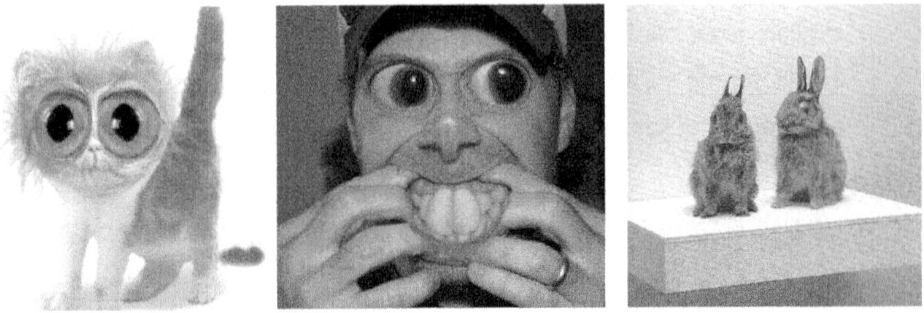

big eyes (*Untitled*, 1996) have been influenced by the popular culture obsession with large pupils as displayed in manga, porno and sci-fi iconography related to biotechnologies? And what do the two big dogs nursing a chick have to share with the popular interest for images documenting bizarre relationships between beasts? Are we really sure that now famous images such as the suicide squirrel (*Bidibidobidiboo*, 1996), the ostrich with his head stuck in the gallery floor (*Untitled*, 1997), the cow with two Vespa handles inserted into its head as horns (*Untitled*, 1997), the donkey with a TV set on its back (*If a Tree Falls...*, 1998), the buried fakir (*Mother*, 1999), the Ku Klux Klan elephant (*Not Afraid of Love*, 2000), and even the kneeling Hitler (*Him*, 2001) and the Pope crushed by a meteorite (*La Nona Ora*, 1999) are only the outburst of Cattelan's imagination and genius? Maybe they come from somewhere else. Maybe he just discovered them, navigating that rich forest of signs that was once the city, and that is now the internet.

Conclusions

To become an image means to abandon the condition in which a work of art is referred to by name, in a usually narrow discursive space, and embrace the condition of those images who everybody knows, usually without knowing what's their name and where they come from. Cattelan was able to reach this goal better than any other artist. Probably this is why most of his works are untitled. His sculptural works are made to be photographed, shared, distributed, commented and manipulated by others. We may go even further, and say that they are born to be used in a demotivational poster. Often they come out from the information flow through casual browsing, looking for such keywords as "squirrel suicide", "sitting donkey", "dead horse". A few artists share the same awareness about the ways images are circulated in the media. Cattelan proved it with his publishing projects, *Permanent Food* and *Toilet Paper*. With his recent retrospective, which is literally invading the internet with its kaleidoscopic photo documentation. [16] With *L.O.V.E* (2010), the first true "memement" in the history of art: a monument born to be photographed, shared, used as an emoticon in a chat, or as a response in an email.

Cattelan inspired internet meme; Maurizio Cattelan, *Bidibidobidiboo*, 1996

But to consider Maurizio Cattelan's work this way may also provide a better ground for understanding the work of a younger generation of artists who grew up in the same information environment, and who relate to it in very similar, or completely different, ways.

This text has been originally written in Italian and published on the website of *Flash Art Magazine* (Italian version) in January 2012 with the title "When an Image Becomes a Work. Premesse a un'iconografia di Cattelan". Translated into English, it appeared on *Pool.info*, May 4, 2012, with the title "When an Image Becomes a Work: Prolegomena to Cattelan's Iconology"

- still available at http://pooool.info/when-an-image-becomes-a-work-prolegomena-to-a-cattelans-iconology/. Two years later, a shorter version of the essay was featured, in English and German, on the columns of the German *Streulicht Magazine*, Issue 5 (Photography-Taboo), November 2014 with the title "Latte Balia: Maurizio Cattelan – The Art of Theft".

[1] This essay has been inspired by a conversation with Eva and Franco Mattes. They first discovered, and pointed to my attention, some of the appropriations discussed in this text. I stole them many ideas, but of course I'm fully responsible of the way I used them. I'm also in debt with Alterazioni Video, who after the publication of this text in Italian sent me some new links.

[2] "Nancy Spector in conversation with Maurizio Cattelan", in VVAA, *Maurizio Cattelan*, Phaidon Press, London – New York 2000. P. 8.

[3] www.targetrichenvironment.net/?p=897.

[4] Nancy Spector (ed.), *Maurizio Cattelan. All*, Guggenheim Museum Publications, New York 2011, p. 241.

[5] According to Massimiliano Gioni, "when he makes his sculptures, Cattelan thinks since the very beginning to their translation into an image. Usually only one image of his sculptures circulates, and it becomes the media version of the work." "In media res". Massimiliano Gioni interviewed by Lucia Longhi, in *Flash Art Italia*, Issue 299, February 2012, p. 34. My translation.

[6] "Nancy Spector in conversation with Maurizio Cattelan", cit., p. 17.

[7] Cf. Jason Huff, "We Copy Like We Breathe: Cory Doctorow's SIGGRAPH 2011 Keynote", in *Rhizome*, August 12, 2011. http://rhizome.org/editorial/2011/aug/12/cory-doctorows-siggraph-2011-keynote/.

[8] Cf. Randy Kennedy, "Apropos Appropriation", in *The New York Times*, December 28, 2011. www.nytimes.com/2012/01/01/arts/design/richard-prince-lawsuit-focuses-on-limits-of-appropriation.html?_r=1.

[9] "Nancy Spector in conversation with Maurizio Cattelan", cit., p. 22.

[10] "Francesco Bonami interviewed by Lucia Longhi", in *Flash Art Italia*, Issue 299, February 2012, p. 31. My translation.

[11] "In media res", cit., p. 34. My translation.

[12] Pierpaolo Ferrari, in Elena Bordignon, "Toilet Paper Magazine", in *Vogue.it*, September 14, 2010, www.vogue.it/people-are-talking-about/art-photo-design/2010/09/toilet-paper-magazine. My translation.

[13] Cf. http://en.wikipedia.org/wiki/Lolcat.

[14] Quoted in *Permanent Food*, Issue 11, 2003.

[15] Cf. www.adaweb.com/context/pf/foam/toc.html.

[16] Francesco Bonami goes even further, saying: "His work is related to the media image. The pictures of the Guggenheim exhibition tell us about a show that doesn't really exist. The museum looks much bigger, the works seem to explode in space [...] But what will remain in memory and in the history of art are the pictures, and thus another show [...] The pictures of the show are the true show, the one the artist imagined, without the technical problems. The ideal show." In "Francesco Bonami interviewed by Lucia Longhi", cit., p. 31. My translation.

Enrico Boccioletti

2012

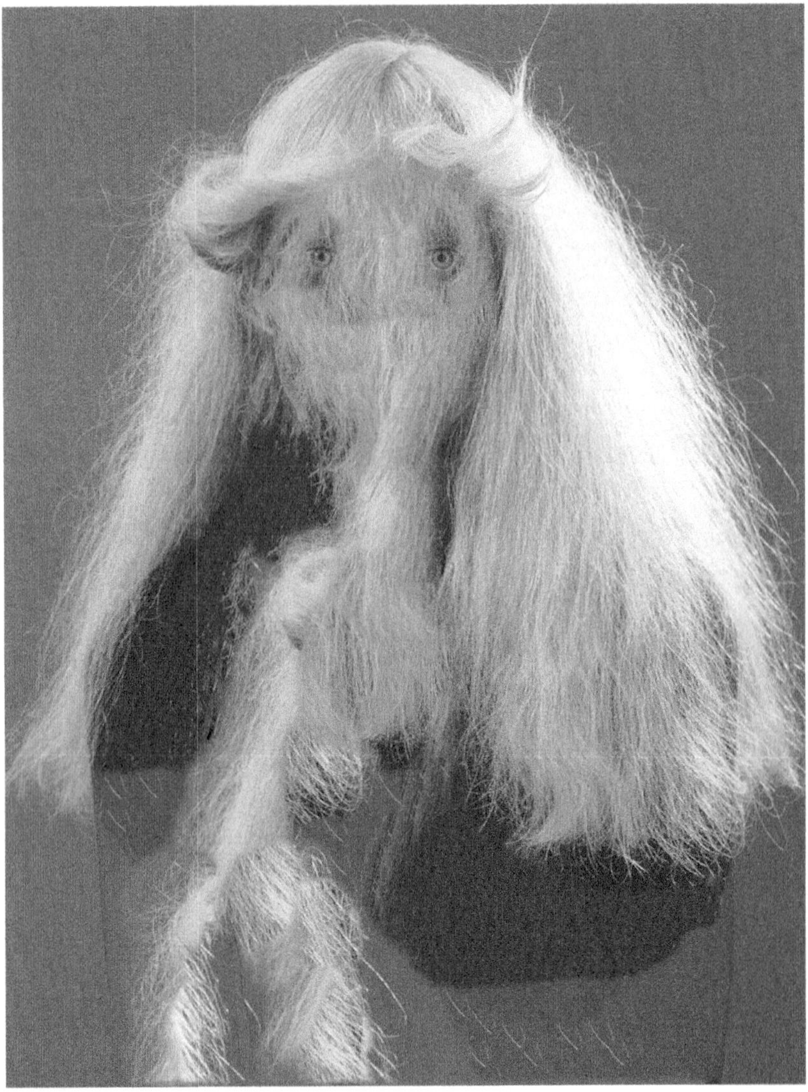

Enrico Boccioletti, *Connie K. Ford, 81 Williams Lane, Wichita, KS 67202* (2012).
Digital print, 29x20 cm. Courtesy the artist

In recent months two incidents have fanned the flames of the ongoing debate on the concept of originality in art. The first was the legal ruling in March 2011 against the artist Richard Prince in a copyright infringement lawsuit brought by the French photographer Patrick Cariou, after Prince used a photographic reportage by Cariou on the Rastafarian community in some of his collages. The second was sparked by a phrase used by the English painter David Hockney in the manifesto of "A Bigger Picture", his solo show at the Royal Academy in London [1]: "All the works here were made by the artist himself, personally." This statement was immediately read as a criticism of Damien Hirst and all the other artists who, like him, often have their work done by assistants.

The debate immediately forked into two opposing factions: "appropriationists" versus "original creators", "producers" versus "designers". In this battle contemporary art has acquired a reactionary, conservative guise: a world of rich, famous artists earning hundreds of thousands of euros from the labours of others, be they "original producers" (like the "poor" Patrick Cariou) whose images they have filched, or the underpaid interns slogging away on "their" works of art. Vice versa, the rebellion against the post-modern and the "old" notion of the artist-creator have acquired an avant-garde flavour. "Enough of Duchamp's idiot offspring! Revisitations are 20th century stuff. Fuck stupid pop art, Warhol and his stupid fucking soup! The new exists. Up with the Avant-garde!", a friend wrote to me commenting on the Prince affair.

There are various holes in the way the debate has been framed. Diametric oppositions like this serve little purpose when we are dealing with a phenomenon as ambiguous, multifaceted and complex as art. There have always been artists who view actually producing art as vitally important, and other artists who rely on helpers, collaborations and the skill sets of others to produce their works. Agnes Martin obviously felt it was crucial for her to trace her own grids, while Damien Hirst reckoned that painting thousands of coloured dots himself would have been a waste of time. Both options are legit, and hardly mutually exclusive. There is no such thing as then and now, old and new. Art is all of this and much more simultaneously.

By the same token, it is becoming increasingly meaningless to oppose appropriationists and creators. Revisitations might well be the stuff of the 20th century, as my friend points out, but there is nothing more 21st century than appropriation. Post modern is dead, but the final nail was not hammered into its coffin by "original creators" à la Cariou, or the law that still remains firmly on their side, but by a combination of three keys that can be found on any computer keyboard: CTRL+C, CTRL+V. The explosion of copy and paste practices has done away with the ideological trappings of appropriation, which has become as natural and immediate as breathing. Previously existing material is not cited or revisited, but used as raw material. As the artist Stephen Frailey says:

> For the generation that I spend my days with, there's not even any ideological baggage that comes along with appropriation anymore.

They feel that once an image goes into a shared digital space, it's just there for them to change, to elaborate on, to add to, to improve, to do whatever they want with it. They don't see this as a subversive act. They see the Internet as a collaborative community and everything on it as raw material." [2]

The reason this is still talked about is because, as the founder of Creative Commons underlines in his book *Free Culture*, the law is moving in the opposite direction, against art and artists. [3] This is result of pressure from music and film industry top brass, but also the claim-staking of those like Cariou, who want a piece of the action – to garner a modicum of the success that their work, on its own merit, would never have achieved.

The reproducibility of digital data, and the ease with which it can be manipulated, have been common knowledge since the dawn of the information era, but the sweeping impact of this on the production and circulation of cultural artefacts has only become evident in the 21st century. Production tools have become increasingly accessible, cheap and easy to use. To manage and display this vast cultural outpouring, a plethora of photo sharing platforms have sprung up, and the production tools have responded to this development by making publication easy and automatic. Ours is the "click and share" society: production is instantaneous and sharing comes immediately after. The licence we decide to use when sharing what we produce is of little importance: those who share take up, manipulate and re-share with equal ease. We break dozens of laws without even realising. All of this regards not only the generation that Stephen Frailey spends his time with: the same principle applies equally to some of the incidents that have most impacted on the social life of the global community in recent years. Take *Wikileaks*, for example: in July 2010 the non-profit organisation published hundreds of confidential military documents regarding the war in Afghanistan, causing the US government and the entire international community more than a spot of bother. None of this would have been possible were it not for the principle that when a piece of information exists in digital form it can be copied (and therefore circulated). And take the "protester" hailed by *Time* magazine as person of the year 2011. The 'Anonymous' movement, that came into being in 2011, is a non-identity shared by hackers, activists and ordinary people who, when protesting against Scientology or global finance, wear a Guy Fawkes mask in honour of the English gunpowder plotter popularised by Alan Moore's comic book and subsequently the Wachowski brothers' film , *V for Vendetta* (2005). And it is an apt mask for a movement that was born on a forum, 4chan, where thousands of people converge to manipulate and comment on images, giving rise to the viral ideas otherwise known as memes.

But if appropriation has become a natural thing, losing the ideological connotations that characterised the Appropriation Art of the 1980s, the conflict between "appropriationists" and "original creators" should be running out of steam by now. Indeed the most interesting work around at the moment is by artists who could be described, not without irony, as skilled in the craft of postproduction. Their modus operandi largely challenges the binary opposition we mentioned at the beginning. Like David Hockney, they do

their own work, but without making this a question of principle. They almost always start their work in front of a computer, fingers moving swiftly over the keyboard. They hardly ever stop there, but the origin is important, because it leaves an indelible mark. Even when the end result is an oil painting on canvas, painted by their own hand or outsourced to a Chinese painting farm.
These are works that come to life in collaboration with one or more software programmes, at times used with a high level of professional skill and at others with nonchalant amateurism, merely deploying default options. They are works that, with equal nonchalance, encompass original creations and material found on the internet. They often arise from dialogue with others, as a response to the work of others. Some are based on collaborative platforms, others actually are collaborative platforms. Sometimes the original materials are left intact and the artist merely selects, collects, classifies and orders them into a collection; while in other instances they are reprocessed to such a degree that it is almost impossible to make out the source material.

Enrico Boccioletti is one such artist, highly skilled in the craft of post production. In his work both as a musician and performer, and as a visual artist, there are no pieces that do not originate elsewhere, in some pre-existing material produced by someone else. Yet it would be a mistake to see him as another Richard Prince. Take *One Month Forkast* (2011) for example, one of his simplest, most radical works. The work consists in an empty site dominated by a static image. Visually it could hardly be more insignificant. The image is the screenshot of a tiny detail of the address bar of a web page, enlarged beyond recognition. What strikes us when we visit it is not the visual aspect of the work, but rather - especially if our computer's speakers are on - the wall of sound, initially intelligible, that rapidly evolves into pure noise. The mechanism is a very simple one. The work consists in a piece of code that retrieves dozens of MP3s from the site of the music magazine Pitchfork, which publishes a podcast entitled Forkast. Specifically, *One Month Forkast* uses the tracks that were made available by Pitchfork in the month the work was created, namely from 25 January to 25 February 2011. All the tracks start up automatically, in random order, at a pace that varies according to a number of external variables: the time of access to the server, the speed of the connection. Although it uses archived material, the work is therefore a performance that takes place live in front of the viewer and that is always different, at every access and to every viewer, though some things remain constant: we are faced with an empty page, following a sound as it is engulfed by an overfull abyss of unsustainable accumulation, generating a noise which results from a stratification of harmonies. Interestingly, Pitchfork is used purely as a tool. The podcast offers sounds from a robust server, nothing more. The operation performed is one of disarming simplicity, yet we perceive a sense of violence, the desire to assault the spectator, rousing us from the state of distracted apathy in which we move from one webpage to another, and to assail music itself, turning it into something more than an irrelevant soundtrack to our everyday activities.

There is a similar brand of aggression, concealed behind a minimal gesture, in the series of prints *Content Aware* (2011). The series takes its name from a function introduced in 2010 in the latest version of Photoshop, [4] the well known photo editing software programme: an "intelligent" algorithm enables the user to remove an element, automatically replacing it with new content which is generated by the programme in accordance with the background. This is how the Photoshop site presents the function:

> **Remove any image detail or object and watch as Content-Aware Fill magically fills in the space left behind. This breakthrough technology matches lighting, tone, and noise so it looks as if the removed content never existed.**

In other words the tool automatises a very complex process, putting it within the reach of any amateur. Bocciolett i makes a fairly banal alternative use of this tool. He appropriates fashion photographs found on the net, selects the area corresponding to the figure or various parts of its anatomy and asks the software to fill in these areas at will. He makes no further modifications. Yet the large size of the selected area and its importance compared to the background creates some problems for the software, which is designed to deal with much smaller areas, causing it to make approximations and mistakes that Bocciolett i accepts as surprising random side effects. In the best case scenario, what is left behind is a light trace, a ghost of the deleted figure, while in the most extreme cases the software generates monsters: bodies without arms or faces, replicated anatomical parts, clothes dressing an empty space, Cubist interiors, eyes staring at us out of wallpaper. Each of these identities annihilated or absorbed into the surrounding setting, yet still present in some way, is given a name, a credible and precise identity by Boccioletti, using a Fake Name Generator found on the internet [5].

Yet again, extremely simple formal strategies are deployed to generate extremely sophisticated result. Boccioletti's images are created for the web, for mass, rapid consumption, the same type of consumption that is the destiny of the fashion photographs he uses as his starting point. By introducing anomalies, the artist in some way rescues them from this brand of consumption, demanding greater attention be devoted to them. His artistic culture also comes into play, drawing bizarre parallels with Western visual art: Impressionist painting, geometric abstraction, hyperrealism, surrealism. He makes them meaningful once more. He forces us to think about their aberrant nature as entities that are part consumer image, part work of art. He adds content.

Originally published with the title "Content Awareness" in *Enrico Boccioletti – Content Aware*, exhibition brochure, Fabio Paris Art Gallery, Brescia, January 2012.

[1] "David Hockney RA: A Bigger Picture". London, Royal Academy, 21 January – 9 April 2012.

[2] Cit. in Randy Kennedy, "Apropos Appropriation", in *The New York Times*, 28 December 2011. Online at www.nytimes.com/2012/01/01/arts/design/richard-prince-lawsuit-focuses-on-limits-of-appropriation.html.

[3] Lawrence Lessig, *Free Culture*, 2004.

[4] The Adobe Creative Suite CS5, launched in February 2010.

[5] Online at http://it.fakenamegenerator.com/.

Constant Dullaart

107

2012

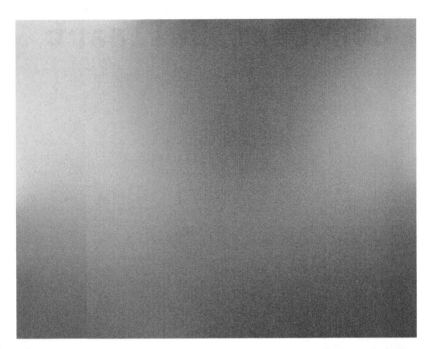

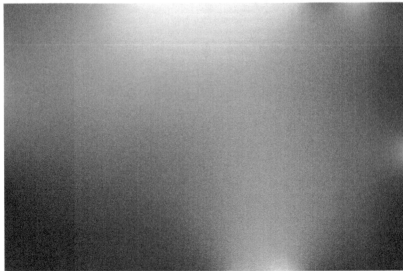

Constant Dullaart, *Re-DeepwaterHorizon_HEALED,* 2011. Video 00:02:13 sec.
Below: Constant Dullaart, *HEALED_Deepwater-article-1031994-01DA767100000578-97_468x306_popup*, 2011. Archival c-print on dibond, 60x80 cm, unique. Courtesy the artist.

Back in the late Sixties, Italian artist Mario Merz took a thin, light blue neon tube, shaped it into a short sentence and placed it into a little black pot. “Che fare?” (“What is to be done?”) is a quote from Lenin, that in its brevity and effectiveness has become a symbol of the hesitation of any revolutionary, when he is forced to choose between theory and action. Merz wasn't the first neither the only artist to use neon signs in his works of art. At the time, this choice was variously interpreted as a reaction against traditional media; against art and its detachment from reality; against commodification of art; and against aesthetics. Labels such as Arte Povera and Conceptual Art mirror these interpretations.

Today, however, another explanation comes to the fore, and seems to make most of the previous ones irrelevant. Using neon lights and signs, Mario Merz, Joseph Kosuth, Dan Flavin and their peers were powerfully criticizing the conventional use of the medium. They were freeing it from its built-in ideology. Neon lights have been conceived to cheaply illuminate badly designed places of alienation like offices and airports. Neon signs are an effective advertisement tool. Using them to convey meaning, or simply to do something different from what they are expected to do is, first and foremost, a reaction against passive acceptation of the habits imposed on us by products and tools, especially by communication tools.

The same insights can be applied, of course, to Nam June Paik's abuse of TV sets, John Cage's misuse of radios, Ed Rusha's exploration of type design, and to most of the art dealing with communication media made between the Sixties and the Nineties, from John Baldessari to Richard Prince, from Cindy Sherman to Jenny Holzer to JODI. In the society of the Spectacle, language is not neutral anymore. Media are designed and commercialized by companies in order to respond to a specific need, to get a certain result, and often to produce new needs that brand new products will satisfy later. Interfaces and software embed the ideas of the programmers who coded them, and of those who asked them to design them that way.

Whatever we say today in a mediated form, it's like a watermarked image from a data bank: it comes with the signature mark of the tool used to say it, be it a mobile phone or a social network, a photo-editing software or a drum machine. There is no easy way out. And so, *Che fare?*

Along the Sixties, for the first time artists realized that language and media didn't belong to them anymore. Reactions spanned from creating new languages and media, to exploring failures and mistakes in commercial media, to appropriation and détournement as tactics of resistance. This way, art acquired a new social function, which is, in my opinion, the main function of art in contemporary society: to set language free, or at least to raise awareness about its current condition. To show that, behind any Photoshop filter, web page design, video effect, game engine there is an ideology; and that any improvement to our ability to communicate also acts as a limitation, an attempt to control, regulate, normalize the signal.

Dutch artist Constant Dullaart takes this mission very seriously, and pursues it with the most simple, effective means. Most of his works might be seen, at a first glance, as easy-to-get one liners, the kind we got tired of, almost a century after Duchamp's *Fountaine*. Readers are warned: don't fall into the trap. Mr. Dullaart is the rare kind of man able to distill a complex content into something as simple as a tweet, a joke, an eye-blink. Take, for example, his series of works dealing with the Google interface:

The Disagreeing Internet (2008): the Google home page moves fast from left to right and back. Available at the URL http://thedisagreeinginternet.com/.

The Doubting Internet (2010): the Google home page tilts left to right and back. Available at the URL http://thedoubtinginternet.com/.

The Sleeping Internet (2011): the Google home page going off and on, fading to black in a way that emulates the behavior of Apple's computers sleeping light, available at the URL http://thedoubtinginternet.com/.

The Revolving Internet (2010): the Google home page rotates full circle, while the browser plays The Windmills Of Your Mind. Available at the URL http://therevolvinginternet.com/.

Internet Spread (2011): the Google home page is split into two pages by a shadowy line in the middle, as if it were a book. Available at the URL http://internetspread.com/.

The Censored Internet (2011): every single word displayed on the Google home page when running a search is censored. Available at the URL http://thecensoredinternet.com/.

All these works display a simple, single behavior. They all deal with the home page of Google, which remains fully functional despite its unorthodox appearance. Whether you first read the domain name, or first focused on the content of the page, when you put them together you get the joke, and you probably smile. And then? Then you leave, maybe a bit disappointed (especially if you where told that this is a work of art), but also richer in a way. You now know, consciously or unconsciously, that Google is not God. That Google is not the absolute, untouchable, clear thing it pretends to be. It censors, and can be censored. It can be displayed upside down. It can disagree, doubt and sleep. *The Revolving Internet* is like Andersen's famous tale, *The Emperor's New Clothes*: when you read it, nothing really changes, except your perception of those in power. Maybe your king is naked, too. Let's make another example. Three early web based works by Constant Dullaart deal with the trope of blowing up something. Visit *blownupbaloon.com* (2008) and you'll first see a white web page. Scrolling the page, you end up seeing some pink, but only if you download the embedded image you'll end up "seeing" the content of the page: a small jpg of a pink baloon, 198x225 px large, blown up to 10120x13029 pixels in order to disappear in the page. The same happens with *blownupexplosion.com* (2008), featuring the picture of an explosion in Iraq, and *blownupblowup.com* (2008), where Michelangelo Antonioni's *Blow Up* (1966) is displayed full page, 10 times bigger than the original file. And here, what comes after disappointment? The joke is, again, revealed by the URL. The content can't be fully experienced and, at least in the first two cases, it has little or no relevance. The three web sites look like wasted domains. Useless web pages. Yet, what is a web page? Anybody who took a lesson of html can tell you that html is a markup language allowing you to build a page, to position elements on it, and to format text. A conventional use of html will bring you to design a conventional web page, where everything is functional to the content: and this is what browser developers want us to do. Displaying a single image and blowing it up in a way that only the title allows us to understand what it is, Dullaart is doing with web pages the same that Mario Merz did with neon signs: he sets the medium free from its conventional, functional use; he makes these conventions visible to everybody; and he proposes another idea of what a website is, or can be.

In the end, most of Constant Dullaart's work is not about software and web sites. It's about companies and media designers taking control on the way we see the word; it's about the way we represent it through languages that they developed, and that we adopt passively, taking advantage of what they allow without caring about what they don't allow us to do, and using their powerful tools without caring about their cultural implications, and their impact on what we say with them.

If you followed me up to this point, you probably already got what's at stake in *Healing* (2010 - 2012). The series includes some pictures and a video, all appropriated from the internet, all picturing a disaster (the infamous Deepwater Horizon oil spill in the Gulf of Mexico, the earthquake in Japan), and all "healed" with the Healing Brush tool offered to us by the latest versions of Photoshop, the most used photo-editing software. The Healing Brush tool has been designed to allow you to correct small imperfections, like spots, causing them to disappear into the surrounding image. It implies that the photo you shot, or the image you scanned, is ill, but it can be easily healed using the right tool. It is, therefore, the by-product of an ideology of post-production, perfecting and falsification, deeply rooted in the software it is part of.

Applying it to the entire image, and to any single frame of the video, Dullaart clearly misuses the software, asking it to do what it wasn't meant for; but he also performs a conceptual leap that allows him to raise many different issues at the same time. Applying the filter to the entire image (and so emphasizing it), and using it to manipulate a news item, Dullaart shows how photography definitely lost its nature of index and proof that something happened, which only survives in our imagination, as a consequence of our inertia and our fear to lose any grasp on reality, and any connection between truth and language. Asking Photoshop to heal reality through its media representation, Dullaart plays with the promises of the software, but also with the widespread belief that, if something doesn't exist as an image, it doesn't exist at all. Last but not least, by playfully subverting the tool and its promises, Dullaart "heals" the medium and the user, providing a different understanding of its potential, limitations and biases.

A final note. Disappointing the audience, as well as reducing the artwork to a single yet powerful gesture, are common strategies in performance art. We already ran out of space, and considering Dullaart's performance based works would go far beyond the limits of this essay. With his irony, his strong personality and his physical presence, Dullaart is doubtlessly a great performer, able to raise awareness about the impact of media on our visual landscape and about the socio-cultural context where the action takes place, be it a museum or a webcam streaming to an online sex video chat service. But the paradigm of performance can be useful also to better understand his work in general, which is innerly performative even when it takes the shape of a website, an installation, a manipulated found image. It usually happens in a public space, the internet; it responds to the media, and it invites you to respond to itself, to complete the process, or to repeat the same gesture again and again. And it does it often successfully, which makes me more hopeful that, in the end, we will maybe succeed in healing the media.

Originally published with the title "Healing the Media" in *Constant Dullaart – Healing*, exhibition brochure, Fabio Paris Art Gallery, Brescia, May 2012.

Jill Magid

2013

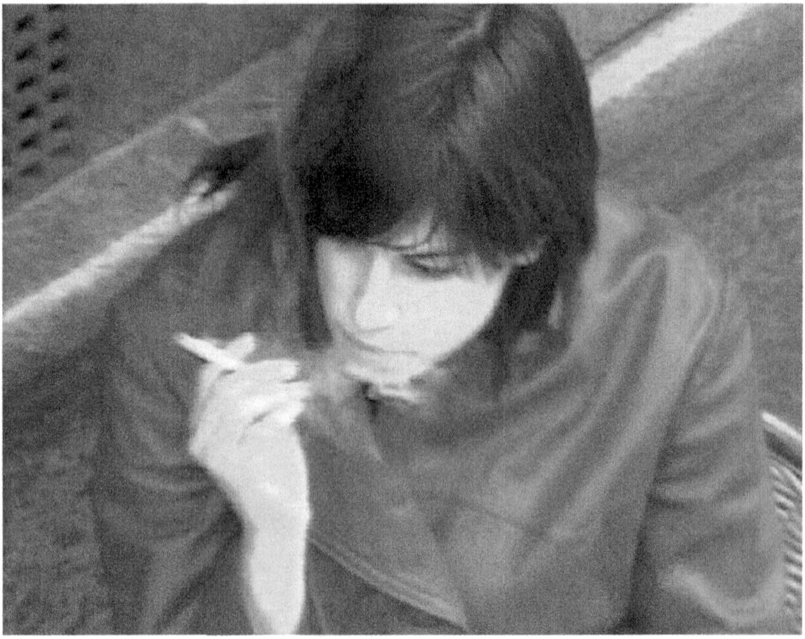

Jill Magid, *Evidence Locker,* 2004. Frame from video, courtesy the artist.

Dear Observer,

Make me a diary and keep it safe. Take care it is mine.

Hold this photograph of my face. Keep all our entries in order.

Put the letters in your desk file and the images in your evidence locker.

You can edit everyone else out.

I will fill in the gaps, the parts of my diary you are missing.

Since you can't follow me inside, I will record the inside for you.

I will mark the time carefully so you will never lose me.

Don't worry about finding me. I will help you. I will tell you what I was wearing, where I was, the time of day... If there was anything distinguishing about my look that day, I will make sure you know.

Hold onto my diary for at least seven years.

I am enclosing a cheque. Use it for whatever expenses you have.

Sincerely,

JSM

On 29 January 2004, Jill Magid arrived in Liverpool, for a 31 day stay. Jill is an artist, and she had been invited to work on a project for the Liverpool Biennial that September. In Liverpool the City Police and City Council had just installed the City Watch System, the largest video surveillance system in the whole of Britain: 242 video cameras dotted around the city centre, a control station with a supervisor and six operators who monitor the city 24/7 on a video wall with 60 screens. The film shot each day is converted into a time-lapse video and stored on the station's computer for 31 days before being destroyed. During that time people can request to see the recordings by filling in a specific form, the "Subject Access Request Form", and paying £10. The material requested is stored in an "Evidence Locker" for at least seven years, while images under judicial scrutiny are archived in the "Jukebox", a digital storage unit in the police's Forensic Imaging Unit. The images stored there are kept forever. Jill Magid already knew all this, after visiting the City Watch control station a few months before, in July 2003, and asking the supervisor to fill in a detailed questionnaire, something he readily did.

This is the framework for Jill's project and the Liverpool Biennial was the catalyst. But this is not a story about bureaucracy, surveillance and art. Rather it is a story of a meeting, a seduction and a love affair; a story in which love and seduction become tools for knowing: "The only way I know a thing is to touch it, and to let it touch me", Jill Magid has declared. The set-up in Liverpool establishes the terms within which Jill and the thing she wants to know can come into contact. They start to get to know one another when they first make that contact.

I did not see you, but was not looking for you yet.
Thursday, January 29, 2004

To get to this point, we have to forgo a lot of supplementary information, and turn the rest into characters and scenarios. Liverpool becomes the "city of L". Jill Magid the artist becomes simply Jill, the girl in the red trench. The "Subject Access Request Form", by means of which material is selected and stored in the Evidence Locker, becomes a love letter. City Watch becomes the Observer, or, simply You. Every day, for 31 days, Jill lives her life in L.: she gets up, has breakfast, goes to the gym, goes jogging, visits exhibitions, attends conferences and meetings, spends an evening with someone, smokes and makes phone calls. And every day, for 31 days, she writes a long letter to the Observer, detailing her movements, talking about her emotions, commenting on their meetings.

> **This morning at 10am I left the house, walked up Rodney, and turned at Hardman Street. I saw you; you did not see me. Your back was turned.**
> **Friday, January 30, 2004**

The narrative that forms around the relationship between Jill and the surveillance system of L. culminates in the humanisation of Observer. Each time Jill says or writes "you", she refers to a part of the system: a camera, a set of cameras, the control room, an operator, the supervisor. Sometimes we can make it out. As we read her letters and analyse the material stored in the Evidence Locker, the Observer begins to take shape, becoming a person. A person with whom Jill forges an intimate relationship built on glances, spoken and unspoken words, dates and let-downs, trust.

> **I stood in the center of the street, in the red coat under my umbrella, and looked at you. I paused and looked right at you.**
> **Saturday, January 31, 2004**

When she looks at a camera, Jill sees eyes. Once humanized, the Observer is no longer a disquieting – or reassuring, depending on how you feel about control – cybernetic organism; it is a person, someone we can relate to along familiar, atavistic dynamics. On 27 February, in her second-last letter, Jill finds herself having to reassure the Observer about the nature of their relationship, writing, "I did not critique your system; I made love to it". In *Evidence Locker* there is no criticism; there is a budding relationship, something new, especially for the Observer. Now a man and a lover, the Observer shows his vulnerable side.

> You marked a path on my map. I followed it. I got a tea at Café Nero and wrote a postcard. You watched me, from two angles, when I did this.
> Sunday, February 1, 2004

This is where the power of *Evidence Locker* lies. The project has been described as belonging to a 'new field of art and activism in which predictable forms of protest against the almighty eyes of power are turned into a dandy-like performance" (Geert Lovink); it has often been compared to the hippy strategy of responding to violence with gestures of peace ("we put flowers in your cannons"). But for Jill the Observer is not an omnipotent Big Brother or an enemy; it is an impersonal structure she sets out to seduce. "I seek intimate relationships with impersonal structures, and prepare for our seduction... Once seduced, a system moves from an exercise of power to a form of exchange."

> How long should I follow you? Just as far as you want to. I would follow you to the end of the world.
> Monday, February 2, 2004

The exchange takes place on an equal footing, and implies trust on both sides. By seducing the system, Jill makes it human and vulnerable. Like any lover, it is naked before her. But her seduction is not part of an attack strategy: this is an authentic love story. There is no faking or deception in her courting. If both parties are looking for something from this affair and find it, that something has nothing to do with their specific role or occupation, but is strictly personal.

> **We fantasize about what we would be, if we were something else than you, an observer and me, a researcher.**
> **Saturday, February 7, 2004**

It is no coincidence that when their customary roles interfere with the story things get awkward. On 12 February Jill is attacked. Three young men on bikes crash into her and yank her bag. This incident is recorded, the men are arrested and Jill goes to the police station to give evidence. She is torn: she feels there is a dissociation between her experience and what the cameras filmed, that she is asked to confirm. The Observer has become a system once more, a system designed to protect civilians, the category Jill belongs to in that moment.

> **I still need to show you Godard's Le Mépris since you have not seen it. I have selected parts of the film for you. Then you will know how to follow me like the camera follows her.**
> **Saturday, February 7, 2004**

There is another awkward moment when, on 27 February, Jill meets the Observer and he questions her, worried, "about this artwork of yours." This question pulls them both back into their usual roles again – the critical artist and the system defending itself from criticism – and the situation has to be handled with great delicacy to get things back on an even keel.

Excluded from the story as an identity, art is an integral part of it as a narrative act. Once she has humanized the Observer, Jill asks him to work with her on a story in which they are both lead character and first person narrator. The story is their love story, the relationship that Jill experiences during her 31 day stay in the city of L. Jill portrays the Observer in her letters; the Observer depicts Jill in the material stored in the Evidence Locker. Like any love story, it takes shape day by day, an interplay of decisions, chance events, alternative perspectives, literary references and narrative devices.

> I liked you telling me how to move; it made me feel more confident, like I was not alone, or the idea was no longer only mine.
> Tuesday, February 10, 2004
> Since this morning I hate the wig and wish I could erase it.
> Tuesday, February 10, 2004
>
> I wanted a coffee and I wanted you to see me. Neither happened.
> Wednesday, February 11, 2004

The story is jointly experienced and written, and their gradually developing intimacy is interspersed with moments of distance, mistakes and misunderstandings, little acts designed to elicit a specific reaction in the other. It is at once banal and extra-ordinary – but extraordinary in a way that is now increasingly inconspicuous: the sensations and emotions traced here for the first time characterise many contemporary love stories. In the age of smartphones and mediated communications, remote surveillance is now a component of most relationships. All lovers are potential Observers. We do not possess the 242 eyes of City Watch, but we have dozens of ways of keeping an eye on our partners. Applications keep track of their last access, and at any time we can check if they have read our last message; are online, and if and how they are handling other social interactions. We observe and are observed. We know when we are being watched, and this awareness conditions how relationships develop. But at the same time, remote communications remain basically obscure, and can have dramatic consequences if they intervene in a relationship that does not have a firm basis of trust. A prolonged silence can become an act of communication that generates doubts and raises questions, eliciting an emotional response. Why isn't he answering? He opened my message 10 minutes ago. Is he busy? Reception problems? Or...

> This place is anonymous; no one knows me; you watch me from above. I am your subject; I relate myself to the city by the way you frame me in it. I know when you see me and when you don't. You can't hear me or smell me or touch me. You know what I wear and where I go. When I pick up the phone, you don't know who is speaking to me, unless I am speaking to you. I like that.
> Thursday, February 12, 2004

What remains extraordinary about Jill's story is that she does not restrict herself to loving through the device, she loves the device itself. And in doing so she understands that building trust is key, and looks straight into the camera. She puts herself out there...

> I will go there, you will come and meet me there, and I will close my eyes and you will hold me. I tell you to search my face. And my body. You want me to search your body? Yes, study me. It does not have to be invasive.
> Friday, February 20, 2004

... and abandons herself to the watching eye.

We were connected, and it was invisible. I told you: I have an idea. I will close my eyes now, and you will walk me there like this.
Saturday, February 21, 2004

In *Trust*, the video that documents this episode, which is both subtle and violent, she surrenders herself to the Observer's arms, and the latter acquires a voice, that is male, warm and reassuring. The process of humanisation is complete and now starts to get personal. Up till now the system, however human, has always manifested itself in plural form: "You" has variously been a man, a woman, a video camera. From that moment on You becomes that specific man: "You, You with a capital Y. You who walks for me. You who I trust completely", as she writes on 27 February. You is on camera himself.

I want to be saved forever.
Tuesday, February 24, 2004

Being in a relationship means writing a story, leaving a trace of one's presence. And writing a story means placing oneself in a more extended time frame. Standing out from the crowd. Becoming an individual, not one among many, and consigning oneself to a longer duration. According to Boris Groys, this is one of the functions of art and the museum: isolating a common object and attributing it a "difference beyond difference", making it last longer than it normally would. According to Jill, this is one of the functions of love: "Love depends on the ability to separate a someone out of the everyone." Or, as she writes to the Observer on 14 February: "I separate you and you separate me." Jill knows that her lover has a special ability to do this for her. 242

cameras are potentially the perfect film set for turning her life in L. into the "Jill Show" and recording every moment. But appearing before the Observer's gaze only guarantees her a duration of 31 days. Using the "Subject Access Request Form" to write the Observer love letters gets her into the Evidence Locker, to be stored in its memory for at least seven years. Getting a copy of the recordings to use in her work consigns her to the potential eternity that Groys talks about. Now part of the permanent collection of the Whitney Museum of New York, *Evidence Locker* has accomplished this aim. By getting the Observer to store some of her images in the Jukebox, Jill has earned herself another kind of forever. "If you ever want to see them, they are in the Jukebox, forever, in a folder with my name, in a folder called February 2004. No rush. I'm permanent."

> **Every time we passed the cameras we waved. And then you said, There is camera number 7. It's the last one we pass.**
> **Saturday, February 28, 2004**

You might think there is nothing more we could want from a love story. But a love story always has something more to give. Jill's love story gives her the chance to take a motorbike ride round the streets of L. She is the passenger while the Observer rides, and together they wave at the surveillance cams before they leave the monitored area. For the first time, albeit temporarily, the Observer is separated from his incessant gaze and the system he embodies and represents. But there's more. This *Final Tour* continues to be recorded by the impersonal but friendly eyes of the cameras, and Jill's writing, informal in style but nevertheless destined to put the last day of her stay in L. into the Evidence Locker. Rather than showing him breaking out of his role, the Observer's escape appears to be a sign of his complete acceptance of the part Jill has asked him to play in her story: observer, lover, narrator, but in turn also a subject for study and observation.

> You said, You know, when you sat on that bench I could have made love to you. And I said, You did.
> Saturday, February 28, 2004

Originally commissioned by Aksioma and published in *Aksioma brochure #15*, Aksioma - Institute for Contemporary Art, Ljubljana, June 2013. Republished in Janez Janša (Ed.), *PostScriptUM #12*, Ljubljana 2014. Online at http://aksioma.org/brochures.

Aram Bartholl

2015

Aram Bartholl, *Keep Alive,* 2015. Sculpture, permanent outdoor installation, image courtesy the artist.

"Walked out this morning / Don't believe what I saw / A hundred billion bottles / Washed up on the shore / Seems I'm not alone at being alone / A hundred billion castaways / Looking for a home"
The Police, "Message in a Bottle", 1979

Back in October 2010, German artist Aram Bartholl cemented 5 USB flash drives in various locations in New York, as part of an Eyebeam residency. [1] Referring to the way, in espionage, items are passed between two individuals using a secret location and without an actual meeting, he called the project *Dead Drops*. The first five dead drops were empty, except for a small readme file explaining the project. A dedicated website was set up, featuring a video tutorial and a simple "how to" and inviting people to participate in the project.

In interviews, Bartholl explained that at the beginning he was just fascinated by the power of an image: a small data container plugged in the wall, in public space, and a person trying to access it with her own device. He invited people to participate by dropping files in and taking files out, installing their own dead drop and sending the GPS coordinates to Bartholl. As in many collaborative projects, he wasn't particularly confident about people's participation, and he believed that the project was conceptually strong enough even in the shape of a small, five-nodes network. But people liked the idea, and as I'm typing on my keyboard today, the online database features almost 1500 registered dead drops for a total storage space of 9891 gigabytes. I installed my own a while ago and I've noticed some others along the years, and I've always been fascinated by the precariousness of these tiny, rusty artifacts. I've never seen anybody plugging in, and probably most of them are almost empty, or out of work. But they are, still, extremely powerful as an image.

Message in a Bottle

> "A Dead Drop is a naked piece of passively powered Universal Serial Bus technology embedded into the city, the only true public space. In an era of growing clouds and fancy new devices without access to local files we need to rethink the freedom and distribution of data. The Dead Drops movement is on its way for change! Free your data to the public domain in cement! Make your own Dead Drop now! Un-cloud your files today!!!"
> Aram Bartholl, "The Dead Drops Manifesto", 2010 [2]

The dead drops network emerged in an age that saw a major shift in the general perception of the internet as a public space. Widespread Wi-Fi access, the massive adoption of social networking sites, and the advent of smartphones made people start to think about the internet as a new public space, with no physical boundaries and infrastructure, where data can be shared and taken easily and seamlessly. The metaphor of the cloud, already used in the Nineties to describe the internet, became more and more popular in the late 2000s, when cloud computing emerged – further reinforcing the idea of an immaterial public space and eroding the difference between public and private, local and shared. As Annet Dekker wrote in 2008:

> "From the time that buildings were first defined as private spaces, the space outside almost automatically served as a public space. Public space referred to the streets, squares and parks of a city. The term public space was a symbol for the spatial and cultural aspects of urban

> life [...] Today the public space is most present on the internet. Through blogs, social networking sites and other online tools, people exchange ideas and public opinions are formulated. The contemporary city has moved into virtual space. A virtual public space that enables forms of sharing and exchange that was [sic!] previously unimaginable." [3]

This "virtual public space", however, was not just an opportunity. Since social networking sites belong to companies, they are more like a mall than a square – with the difference that in this virtual mall you are not invited to buy products, but you are the product. The kind of surveillance you experience there is not just meant to protect you (or society from you), but to turn your data (the images you share, the words you write, the things you do) into commodities to be sold to other companies. The impact of this on our concepts of privacy and property has been tremendous – and cloud computing made these concepts even more ambiguous and vague. With cloud computing, you get online storage space that can easily be accessed from any networked device you use. This storage space is protected by a username and a password, and is thus perceived as private, but it isn't. Not just because this protection can be easily cracked by hackers; but because the server space doesn't belong to you; its usage is regulated by terms and conditions that are often changed by the service provider; and its content (in the form of digital files), even if it was regularly bought and paid for, is not owned like material forms of private property, and regulated by third party agreements that may change any time.

Dead Drops was one of the first artist projects pointing to these issues, as the manifesto makes clear when it talks about the city as "the only true public space" and invites people to "uncloud" their files. It didn't stress these topics just by means of criticism, although the criticism was very clear. No surprise that, along the last five years, the project experienced various waves of interest, both in terms of media attention and in terms of public usage. From the debate around the Pirate Bay and Megaupload, to the protests against ACTA, from Wikileaks to the Snowden revelations, from the theft and circulation of personal data of celebrities stored in their cloud accounts to some Anonymous stunts, to name just a few stories that hit the headlines, the issues of property and privacy in the "virtual public space" have become major topics of public debate.

Dead Drops didn't provide a viable, realistic alternative to online file sharing and to cloud computing either. Every "port" is also a dead end, and can only be accessed on site. The storage space is limited (most often, to 4 or 8 GB). Every single user has complete control over the content of the dead drop at hand: she can delete all the files, add useless or meaningless stuff, install viruses, damage the device, remove it. The device itself is subject to physical deterioration and weather conditions.

7,000 Oaks

What *Dead Drops* really offered, and what made (and still makes) it successful, was the possibility to deliver a signal and to make a small, yet effective, intervention, by means of a powerful image and a very simple process. When you encounter the project, by word of mouth, on the internet, or just wandering through the city, it's pretty easy to get some of its cultural implications. If you agree with these implications, you don't even need Bartholl's invitation to install your own dead drop in order to do it: this invitation is somehow embedded in the intervention itself. When you see it, and agree with what it says, there is only one way to amplify its message: install your own dead drop. It's simple, cheap, playful; it allows you to publicly express your ideas – just like wearing a pin or raising a banner – and it gives you the additional pleasure of any small illegal act – just like placing a sticker or replicating a piece of graffiti. But installing a dead drop is not just a symbolic gesture. By doing it, you donate some small digital storage space you own to the public realm. It may be useless and ineffective, it may go unnoticed, it may be stolen or get broken. But it's there. You did it. Somebody, for any purpose, may actually use it. Hundreds and thousands of dead drops do not just work on a symbolic level: they generate an amount of offline, anonymous, public storage space. They create an infrastructure. It may take time to realize how to use it, but it's there, and it's a resource.

A comparison with another public social sculpture – and a seminal project in the genre – may be useful at this point. In 1982, on the occasion of *Documenta 7*, German artist Joseph Beuys had 7,000 basalt stones brought from a quarry outside Kassel to the lawn in front of the Fridericianum, Documenta's principal exhibition building. According to his plan, the stones would have been completely removed from the site only when *7,000 oaks* had been planted around the city – "each paired with a columnar basalt marker measuring approximately four feet above ground". [4] According to Lynn Cooke's account,

"The action continued over the next five years under the aegis of the Free International University, the diminishing pile of stones in front of the Fridericianum indicating the progress of the project. Planting in public spaces in the inner city was carried out on the basis of site proposals submitted by residents, neighborhood councils, schools, kindergartens, local associations, and others. [...] At the opening of Documenta 8 in June 1987, some eighteen months after his father's death, Beuys's son Wenzel planted the last tree." [5]

In various statements released about the project, Beuys explained:

"I believe that planting these oaks is necessary not only in biospheric terms, that is to say, in the context of matter and ecology, but in that it will raise ecological consciousness – raise it increasingly, in the course of the years to come, because we shall never stop planting. [...] The planting of seven thousand oak trees is thus only a symbolic beginning. And such a symbolic beginning requires a marker, in this instance a basalt column. The intention of such a tree-planting event is to point up the transformation of all of life, of society, and of the whole ecological system..." [6]

On a symbolic level, the project wanted to raise ecological awareness to a level that would bring people to keep planting trees not as a way to participate in Beuys' social sculpture, but as a consequence of their own beliefs. On a functional level, the project wanted, locally, to have an impact on the presence of green areas in city planning; and globally, it sought to have an environmental impact, that would be minimal at the beginning but consistent for the world that future generations would be living in.
While *7,000 Oaks* wanted to change our future eco system, *Dead Drops* has the ambition to change our future informational environment, both symbolically and functionally, by raising a new in-

formational awareness and providing an infrastructure based on a vision that is different from the one shared by the companies and institutions that are currently shaping the internet.
But what is the internet? And does it even exist?

The Internet Does Not Exist

> “The internet does not exist. Maybe it did exist only a short time ago, but now it only remains as a blur, a cloud, a friend, a deadline, a redirect, or a 404. If it ever existed, we couldn’t see it. Because it has no shape. It has no face, just this name that describes everything and nothing at the same time. Yet we are still trying to climb onboard, to get inside, to be part of the network, to get in on the language game, to show up on searches, to appear to exist. But we will never get inside of something that isn’t there. All this time we’ve been bemoaning the death of any critical outside position, we should have taken a good look at information networks. Just try to get in. You can’t. Networks are all edges, as Bruno Latour points out. We thought there were windows but actually it’s made of mirrors.” [7]

The editors of the *e-flux journal* are not the first to make this point. In *The Net Delusion*, [8] Russian writer and researcher Evgenij Morozov insists that we should stop speaking about “the Internet” as a subject with its own intentionality and personality, because such a subject doesn’t exist. The internet is just a technical infrastructure, constructed and perused by different people with different ideas and intentions, and with features that are neither good nor bad, but that can be used either for good or for bad. But the point that e-flux’s editorial board make is actually stronger: what they put into question is the very existence, or, better, the possibility to define, this infrastructure. It may, they argue, have existed in the past: but the way it evolved over the decades, and especially in the late nineties, when commercial interests came in, makes it impossible to find a definition for what the internet is at the present time. And yet, at the end of their introduction, they present a more positive perspective:

> "[...] contradictions don't resolve, rather you surf across them using empathy and solidarity, emotional blackmail, jokes, pranks, and vanguardism as norm. Our ability to traverse these contradictions may very well become the backbone of the global telecommunications network we used to think was an internet. [9]

At the rise of social networking, a number of critical projects were developed by artists and activists, commenting on, questioning and often interfering with the way they were overtaking the internet. To categorize these projects and contextualize the way in which resistance should be structured against the way social networks are redefining our approach to sociality, media theorist Geoff Cox coined the term "antisocial notworking". Cox explains:

> "The plurality of nodes in networks does not guarantee a more inherent democratic order; indeed it arguably serves to obscure its totalitarian substructure. This is the trick of social networking in offering the promise of democracy but though centralized ownership and control where the web platform itself mediates relations (unlike peer to peer file sharing for instance) [sic!]." [10]

And, quoting Maurizio Lazzarato:

> "If production today is directly the production of a social relation, then the 'raw material' of immaterial labor is subjectivity and the 'ideological' environment in which this subjectivity lives and reproduces. The

production of subjectivity ceases to be only an instrument of social control (for the reproduction of mercantile relationships) and becomes directly productive, because the goal of our postindustrial society is to construct the consumer/communicator – and to construct it as 'active'. [...] The fact that immaterial labor produces subjectivity and economic value at the same time demonstrates how capital has broken down all the oppositions among economy, power, and knowledge." [11]

This is one of the many underlying forces that turned "the internet" into that blurry, amorphous non-entity we experience today. While along the years many artists addressed these topics adopting affirmative or over-affirmative [12] strategies – from Petra Cortright turning herself into a YouTube star, to Eva and Franco Mattes exploiting crowd workers and using more or less obscure video sharing platforms to distribute the content produced in their recent project *BEFNOED* (2014) [13] – "anti-social notworking" mostly identifies projects that adopt a critical, more straightly subversive approach, and that often offer an alternative that may be either imaginative or useful. A good example is provided by two classics in the genre: *GWEI* (*Google Will Eat Itself*, 2005) and *Amazon Noir* (2006), developed by the Austrian couple UBERMORGEN in collaboration with Alessandro Ludovico and Paolo Cirio. [14] *GWEI* portrays the impossible, titanic effort, performed by a smaller, fictional company called *GWEI*, to turn Google into a publicly owned company by buying Google shares with the income provided by Google Ads, and donating them to another, publicly owned company called GTTP (Google To The People). The project produces a rift in "Google's porcelain interface" by portraying the absurdity of a huge private company ruling and controlling access to the internet, mostly perceived as a public space; and offers a solution that, although impossible in the short term, is technically viable. In the narrative of the second project, *Amazon Noir* is a parasitic company that steals books from Amazon and releases them on peer-to-peer networks, exploiting a bug in Amazon's "Search Inside the Book" function. This time, the story told is that of copyright and commercial interests versus free circulation of knowledge. The theft was stopped when Amazon noticed the activity of the software the group used to grab content from the books pdfs; [15] but again, the attempt was not to offer an effective alternative, but to make clear that such an alternative is at least conceivable; that the internet is something we build, and that it can be very different from whatever it has become today.

Alt Internetz

> "Web-based service providers such as Facebook and Google are not the Internet, but rather are web-based platforms built on the Internet. The superior user-experience of such services accrues a dedicated user base for basic communication functionalities. The design idiosyncrasies of these platforms define popular culture. However just because certain service providers have become dominant does not mean that the techniques or strategies they employ are fundamentally superior. These have become dominant because they have evolved a business model which ensures a generous ROI. Without exception, the leading platforms ensure value for their investors by trading in user data." [16]

These words, written by Baruch Gottlieb and published on the Telekommunisten website, open up new perspectives on the future of the internet. What, at first glance, may look like a permanent involution of the social platform once provided by the internet, is instead the temporary state of a complex ecosystem shaped by humans. Alternative internets are possible, even if at the moment they can only be imagined, or take the shape of a small art project. Gottlieb goes on:

> "There are myriad ways to use the Internet, there are myriad different paradigms for Internet-enabled communication, collaboration and other social activities which can and are being explored. Whether or not they can 'compete' with the Googles and Facebooks, depends today entirely on whether they can produce sufficient 'surplus value' to satisfy investors, thereby to attract sufficient funding to produce superior user experience. In all the world wide web there is not a model for this which is not centered on the harvesting and analysis of user data." [17]

Even if, in this paragraph, the optimism of the first lines is undermined by the belief that only investors can turn a good idea into a new working model, what's interesting for us in this context are these "myriad different paradigms for Internet-enabled communication, collaboration and other social activities". In their own work, Telekommunisten have worked on the concept of "miscommunication technologies". As they explained in a lecture:

> "Communications technologies embody and perpetuate the social relations of their mode of production. The Miscommunication Technologies series of artworks by Telekommunisten explore these social relations by creating technologies that don't work as expected, or work in unexpected ways. The artworks in the series allow the embedded social relations to be critically experienced and confronted. The series employs parody, juxtaposition, exaggeration and reductio ad absurdum to bring aspects of these relations which are normally hidden from view, into the foreground." [18]

A good example of such a miscommunication technology is *OCTO P7C-1* (2013), a pervasive pneumatic tube network set up by OCTO, a fictional venture capitalist-sponsored start-up that promises to build the next dimension of the internet. Conceived as an installation for large exhibition spaces, *OCTO P7C-1* is fully functional although allowing, of course, only in-site communication exchange between people. Sending a message is purposefully complicated, and the management of information is fully exposed, in a sharp contrast with what happens on the internet whose materiality is usually hidden, and where physical labor is invisible and the flow of information fast and seamless. *Thimbl* (2010), on the other side, is a fully functional, distributed, peer-to-peer alternative to microblogging platforms such as Twitter, presented as an online service built upon an open protocol developed in the 1970s and called "Finger". But instead of providing a utopian, community-based alternative to commercial platforms, *Thimbl* translates into a piece of software the cynical belief of Telekommunisten that

> "For Thimbl, or any other platform with a similar vision, to become a real alternative to the capitalist financed platforms like Facebook and Twitter, we need more than running code, even more than a small, perhaps dedicated, user base. To get beyond this and actually break the monopolizing grip of centralized social media we need to match their productive capacities. We need financing on a similar scale. [S]o that the development, marketing, and operations budgets are comparable and sufficient to compete. [...] [F]or economic fiction like Thimbl to become reality society will need to transcend the political and economic limitations that we currently face. We can write code, we can write texts, we can create artworks, but as a small network of artists and hackers, we can't change the economic conditions we work in by ourselves." [17]

And yet, every message in a bottle is also a proof that there is room left for hope. In 2014, American artist Trevor Paglen developed, in collaboration with computer security researcher and hacker Jacob Appelbaum, *Autonomy Cube*, a sculpture designed to be housed in art museums, galleries, and civic spaces, creating an open Wi-Fi hotspot called "Autonomy Cube" wherever it is installed. But instead of providing a normal internet connection, the sculpture routes all of the Wi-Fi traffic over the Tor network, a global network of thousands of volunteer-run servers, relays, and services designed to help anonymize data. In addition, the sculpture is itself a Tor relay, and can be used by others around the world to anonymize their internet use. Usually perceived as the infamous access door to the Darknet, Tor is here presented and used for what it is in the first place: a huge community effort interested in preserving the privacy of its users, instead of capitalizing on it.
In 2012, Rui Guerra and David Jonas developed *Uncloud*, a small gesture of software resistance against the cloud:

> "unCloud is an application that enables anyone with a laptop to create an open wireless network and distribute their own information. Once it is launched, a passerby using a mobile internet device can connect to this open wireless network. The person running the application can decide what information is shown in any web address. Users can access information wirelessly while at the same time remain disconnected from the internet. unCloud does not depend on a remote datacenter, instead it can be run from a laptop, making it an ideal application to run in a train or at a café." [18]

UnCloud does not offer what the cloud offers in terms of external storage space and accessibility from wherever in the world and from any device; but it allows you to protect your data while simultaneously sharing them with a small, localized community. It invites us to think about the pros and cons of having every content we produce available on the internet, and to consider the option of "unclouding" them when the reason why we are putting them online can be better served by other, offline services.

Keep Alive

Aram Bartholl's *Keep Alive* (2015) is a land art project commissioned by the Leuphana Arts Program and located in the outdoor premises of Kunstverein Springhornhof in Neuenkirchen, Germany. The piece offers access to a big digital library containing a collection of survival guides of any kind – from classical survival guides to Photoshop tutorials – through a local wi-fi access point activated by fire. The library can be accessed via a wi-fi router that is located in a big boulder and powered by a TEG (thermo electric generator). When you make a fire next to the boulder, the heat activates the TEG generator, which then turns on the wi-fi. The network is on only as long as the metal plate of the TEG is heated up.

The title, *Keep Alive*, refers to the keepalive signal, a message – often sent at predetermined intervals – that is used on networks to check the link between two devices, to make a diagnosis or to indicate to the internet infrastructure that the connection should be preserved. In the economy of the work, it also points to the fact that the fire has to be kept alive in order to keep the network running.

The piece generates a fiction that ironically locates it in a post-apocalyptic, cyberpunk scenario where humanity has been "kept alive", the internet is over and power is provided by fire, but also where technologies and pieces of information have survived as digital junk. Presented as an artwork and preserved as such, it may once turn useful and even essential for a wandering Mad Max to survive, as the only remaining access point to basic information. As such, the project shares a lot with the rusty dead drops network: what is now mostly a mind meme and a social game may, in a dystopic scenario, turn into a fundamental infrastructure for data exchange. At the same time, however, as every archive or library that survived from a long-lost past, *Keep Alive* is also a time capsule preserving a knowledge responding to needs that may not be there in the future. Maybe, in this scenario, knowing how to photoshop an image would still be a matter of survival; but what about the usefulness of the fashion survival guide, the teaching my first class survival guide or the post-internet survival guide, for the matter?
Like *Dead Drops*, and many other works presented here, Keep Alive is an attempt to visualize the physicality of a network infrastructure, and to translate the immateriality of information transfer and online sociality into physical visual metaphors that can be presented in the so-called "real world": a concern that has accompanied Aram Bartholl through all his career, from workshop-based projects like *WoW* (2006 – 2009) to new exhibition formats like *Speed Show* (2010 – ongoing) and *Offline Art* (2013), from monumental public installations like *Map* (2006 – 2013) to his recent gallery work.

Furthermore, and similarly to Paglen and Appelbaum's *Autonomy Cube*, *Keep Alive* can be seen as an attempt to "promote" – quotation marks are obviously required here – within the framework of the art world (and so, in a cultural context that is very different from the one that generated it), a powerful alternative to mainstream technology, and to show its potential for setting up alternative communication systems. The wi-fi router used for *Keep Alive* is the PirateBox, a DIY anonymous offline file-sharing and communications system built with free software and inexpensive off-the-shelf hardware. The PirateBox creates offline wireless networks designed for anonymous file sharing, chatting, message boarding, and media streaming. In other words, it's a kind of "portable offline Internet in a box". It has been conceived by artist, coder and designer David Darts, and it's not for sale, but is a DIY project that can be built by the user following simple instructions. Significantly, Darts declared that the project was inspired, among other things, by the *Dead Drops*. [19]

But first and foremost, *Keep Alive* is – like all the works discussed here – a work of art and a tool for social change: a piece of matter that works mostly on a symbolic level, but that's also potentially useful. Like an oak planted close to a basalt stone. Or a message in a bottle, dropped into the sea and waiting to get into the hands of the unknown somebody who knows what to do with its content.

Commissioned in May 2015 by the Center for Digital Cultures, Leuphana University Lüneburg. First published in *Media In the Expanded Field*, May 12, 2016, with the title "Oh, When the Internet Breaks at Some Point". Available online at https://mefsite.wordpress.com/2016/05/12/domenico-quaranta-oh-when-the-internet-breaks-at-some-point/.

[1] Eyebeam is a leading not-for-profit art and technology center in the United States. Founded in 1997 in New York, Eyebeam hosts, among other things, a 5 months residency conceived as "a period of concentration and immersion in artistic investigation, daring research or production of visionary, experimental applications and projects." Cf. http://eyebeam.org/programs/creative-residencies.

[2] Aram Bartholl, "The Dead Drops Manifesto", 2010. Online at https://deaddrops.com/dead-drops/manifesto/.

[3] Annet Dekker, "PPS: PublicPrivateSpace. Where the public space turns into private space and the private space opens up to the public", 2008, in VVAA, *Proceedings of ISEA2008. The 14th International Symposium on Electronic Art*, 25 July – 3 August 2008, Singapore.

[4] Cf. Lynn Cooke, "7,000 Oaks", Dia Art Foundation 1995 – 2004. Online at http://web.mit.edu/allanmc/www/cookebeuys.pdf.

[5] Ibid.

[6] Ibid.

[7] Julieta Aranda, Brian Kuan Wood, Anton Vidokle (Eds), *The Internet Does Not Exist*, Sternberg Press, April 2015. The editorial introduction is also available online at http://www.e-flux.com/books/the-internet-does-not-exist/.

[8] Evgenij Morozov, *The Net Delusion: The Dark Side of Internet Freedom*, Public Affairs 2012.

[9] Julieta Aranda, Brian Kuan Wood, Anton Vidokle (Eds), *The Internet Does Not Exist*, cit.

[10] Geoff Cox, "Antisocial Applications: Notes in Support of Antisocial Notworking", in *Vague Terrain*, Issue 11, September 2008, online at http://vagueterrain.net/journal11/geoff-cox/01.

[11] Ibid.

[12] Cf. Inke Arns, Sylvia Sasse, "Subversive Affirmation. On Mimesis as a Strategy of Resistance", in IRWIN (Ed), *East Art Map. Contemporary Art and Eastern Europe*, Cambridge: MIT Press / London: Afterall, 2006, pp. 444-455: "Subversive affirmation and over-identification – as 'tactics of explicit consent' – are forms of critique that through techniques of affirmation, involvement and identification put the viewer/listener precisely in such a state or situation which she or he would or will criticise later. What the various tactics and parasitical practices have in common is that they employ the classical aesthetical methods of: imitation, simulation, mimicry and camouflage in the sense of 'becoming invisible' by disappearing into the background."

[13] The artists sent to anonymous people working for crowdsourcing platforms simple instructions to make a webcam performance, often inspired to the absurd, minimal gestures that sometimes generate internet memes; the same set of instructions was sent to different people, and various performances have been implemented. By distributing them – without an art label on them – on sharing platforms and social networks mostly used in third world countries, the Mattes explore their effects on unaware audiences. The title is an acronym for "By Everyone For No One Every Day". Cf. http://befnoed.tumblr.com/.

[14] Cf. www.ubermorgen.com/EKMRZ_Trilogy/

[15] The "Search inside the book" function allows the Amazon customer to see small samples of a book that is available online in its entirety, but hidden under a mask that the software built by the group was able to circumvent, grabbing page after page and collecting them in a single text file. For more info, see www.amazon-noir.com/.

[16] Baruch Gottlieb, "The Internet is not a Surveillance State...", March 27, 2013, online at http://telekommunisten.net/2013/03/27/the-internet-is-not-a-surveillance-state/.

[17] Ibid.

[18] Dmytri Kleiner, Baruch Gottlieb, "Miscommunication Technologies. Telekommunisten Artworks 2009-2013", August 21, 2014, online at www.dmytri.info/miscommunication-technologies-with-dmytri-baruch-at-berlinatonal/.

[17] Ibid.

[18] Cf. www.intk.com/en/ideas/uncloud.

[19] For more information, cf. http://piratebox.cc/.

Émilie Brout and Maxime Marion

149

2015

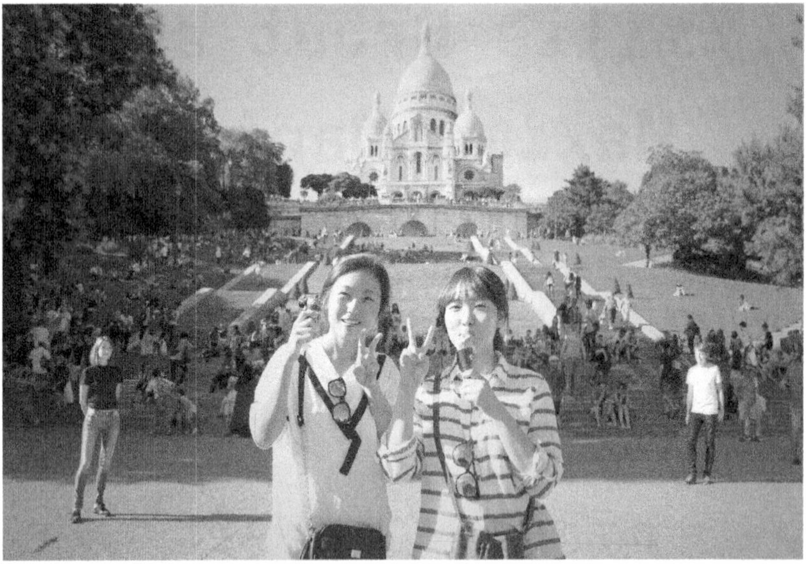

Émilie Brout and Maxime Marion, *Ghosts of your Souvenir,* 2014 - ongoing,
Installation, 80 x 280 cm, collection of found onlline photographies, digital print on plexiglas, dibond. Image courtesy 22,48 m^2, Paris

In the Oxford English dictionary, value is primarily defined as "the regard that something is held to deserve; the importance, worth, or usefulness of something". In the Merriam-Webster, "a fair return or equivalent in goods, services, or money for something exchanged" comes first, underlying the prominence of economics in the age of capitalism. Both definitions, however, agree on one thing: setting a value for something is more a matter of agreement than objectivity. How can you say that a return is "fair"? That something is regarded as much as it deserves?

In today's post-capitalist, post-digital, post-whatever societies, moreover, both these definitions look outdated. Today, value is much more unstable, much more ephemeral, much more liquid than this. And it's, more often than not, unfair. How much is worth one minute of labor? How much is worth the future? How much is worth Greece? How much is worth a company trading in information? How much is worth a single piece of information? How much is worth attention? How much is worth a work of art? Each of this things, the very same thing, may vary on a scale from 0 to 1 billion something. The value of information, attention and works of art is so unstable that, very properly, they have become currencies themselves.

The meaning of value in a post-whatever era, the mass abundance of images – from amateur image production to professional images to algorithmically generated images – and the consequent shift of the artist from production to post-production – and from the creation of works to the generation of formats – are all recurring topics in the recent work of Émilie Brout and Maxime Marion. Since 2009 the French couple has been focusing on projects that, renovating the modernist language of film, make an extensive use of appropriated content from the web, which is freed from its status of meaningless, apparently valueless data floating in the information networks to be rearranged in complex, algorithmically generated, sometimes interactive narratives, or into powerful, iconic images.

In this context, the foundation of *Untitled SAS* (2015) may look like a smart yet radical move out of this line of research, while it is, in fact, a further step in the same direction, though less visual and more conceptual. In French, SAS stands for "société par actions simplifiées", the equivalent of a registered limited company (LTD or INC in English). *Untitled SAS* is an immaterial work of art whose medium is a company business, with "work of art" as corporate purpose and with a capital open to everybody interested in buying shares at their own price. The starting capital of the company is set to 1,00 € (the minimum legally possible), and 10,000 shares are made available. With a freely negotiable capital, the company allows each collector/shareholder to buy and sell shares at the price he set, thus influencing the company's overall value (displayed on a dedicated website).
In order to set up the company, the artists worked with one of the largest and oldest lawyer's office of Paris, Granrut Avocats, who had to resolve many new legal paradoxes for its official registration in the French Trade and Companies Register. A similar gesture was performed, years ago, by the Austrian-Swiss collective etoy, who registered themselves as an actual company in Switzerland, with making art as its corporate purpose. But while etoy, in the early years of the internet, were embracing – in an over-affirmative way – the utopian dream of the new economy in order to set them free

from the rules of the art market, Emilie Brout and Maxime Marion are more interested in giving birth to a useless yet fully functional machine that performs and mirrors the ways of working of the current art market, where the value of artworks looks less rooted in the material value of the object or in the cultural value of the work, and more in the ability of a few disruptive characters to manipulate it at their will. At the same time, however, as a socially owned, immaterial artwork with a starting value set to the minimum and able to increase with the help of a community of collectors/shareholders, *Untitled SAS* is the archetypal work of art: like a medieval church, it mirrors and represents the power in charge, while at the same time being available for the larger society. It also bears some spiritual connotations, recalling the *Zones of Immaterial Pictorial Sensibility* (1959) by Yves Klein: the empty space exchanged for gold is replaced by the empty shell of a company turned into shares. Finally, it is the perfect portrait of companies like Facebook, that started valueless and evolved into modern golden calfs.

In such companies, value is mostly generated by their ability to attract users, to welcome user generated content that draws in other users, and to capitalize on their private data: which turns amateur cultural production and privacy into two key issues to understand the present day. In this context, Emilie Brout and Maxime Marion often become modern gold diggers involved into what David Joselit called "an Epistemology of Search". This can be seen in many works on show, including *Regulus*, *Ghosts of Your Souvenirs* (2014 – ongoing), *Les Nouveaux chercheurs d'or* and *Return of the Broken Screens* (2015). *Regulus* is a generative animation based on a program that browses websites like Flickr, Instagram and Google Images in real time, in search of pictures that respond to some formal criteria then used to organize the visual flow. While the focus of their interest – the presence of round shapes – takes center stage, the main subject of these pictures – and the reason why they have been shared in the first place – fades in the background without disappearing completely, being perceived as a background noise or a flow of subconscious images. The piece also shares with *Untitled SAS* an experimental attitude toward how cultural value is translated into market value: instead of being sold as a unique or an edition, this ever evolving piece is chunked into small samples and sold by weight.

Like *Regulus*, *Ghosts of Your Souvenirs* is an ongoing collection of found amateur pictures where the main subject becomes secondary when the viewer understands the organizing principle of the collection: the presence, in the background, of Emilie or Maxime (or both), posing for a photographer who's not interested in them. In order to develop the project, the artists stood for one or more days in a chosen place of touristic interest – on the Rialto Bridge in Venice, or in front of Notre Dame de Paris – trying to be featured in as many tourist photos as possible; and later spent hours on image sharing sites like Instagram and Flickr, looking for images taken that day in that place. The collection thus becomes an outsourced self portrait, that takes advantage of the ubiquity of the camera eye, the seamlessness of sharing and the informational nature of digital images, all equipped with their metatags.

If *Regulus* and *Ghosts of Your Souvenir* deal with the explosion of amateur cultural production, other works in the show are a take on online economics. *Les Nouveaux chercheurs d'or* is an ongoing collection of free golden samples of golden products sold on the internet. Gold is a universal symbol of value, and a way to turn any prosaic, mass produced item into something shiny and desirable. By collecting these samples, Emilie Brout and Maxime Marion are interested in the conflict between their luxurious look, their free nature and the complexity of the economics that produced them, that they research in depth, trying to provide as much information as possible about the collected item.

This interest in the background story of the collected pieces is shared by *Return of the Broken Screens*, based on a collection of broken display technologies. Commercially speaking, tech items are valuable when they work, and totally valueless when broken. A small incident can turn an expensive gadget into something you are lucky if you don't have to spend money to get rid of it. But a small incident can also be an interesting story; and a damaged display is just another kind of display. That's why Emilie and Maxime research into these stories and create customized abstract videos for these displays, responding to their cracks and choosing shapes and colors according to their ability to activate a given part of the screen – fully aware that the decay will go on and that the work in the present form will be short lived.

Actually, most of the works by Emilie Brout and Maxime Marion have a performative nature that makes the work displayed in the gallery appear as the temporary, inevitably limited instantiation of an ongoing process, rather than a finished piece. This is literally true for *Nakamoto (The Proof)*, 2014 – 2015, an attempt to produce a portrait of the legendary founder of Bitcoin using the economic and technical system he gave birth to as a "brush". Bitcoin is a virtual currency widely used on "darknets" like the Tor network, and allowing to perform online transactions anonymously. Despite (or thanks to?) its virtual nature, during the financial recession its value has grown up constantly, and it has been perceived as a safe-haven asset. With an estimated fortune of several hundred million euros, Satoshi Nakamoto still lives in the grey zone between fiction and reality, thanks to his ability to preserve his identity. After collecting all the available information about Nakamoto, Emilie Brout and Maxime Marion browsed Tor in order to get in touch with a group of passport forgers, probably based in Cambodia, and commissioned them a fake passport of Nakamoto, in the attempt to produce an evidence of his existence using the technology he created. After getting a scan of the passport for validation, they paid the second instalment and the passport was shipped on June 7, 2014, but it was never delivered to them, the scan still being the only evidence of its existence. Unavailable as an artifact, as a story *Nakamoto (The Proof)* works as a research into the folds of contemporary economics, and a tribute to a modern myth that was both able to reinvent value as well as to preserve himself to be turned into a product.

Originally commissioned by 22,48 m², Paris and first published with the title "Les Nouveaux chercheurs d'or" in *Émilie Brout and Maxime Marion – Les Nouveaux chercheurs d'or*, exhibition catalogue, 22,48 m², Paris 2015.

Evan Roth

157

2016

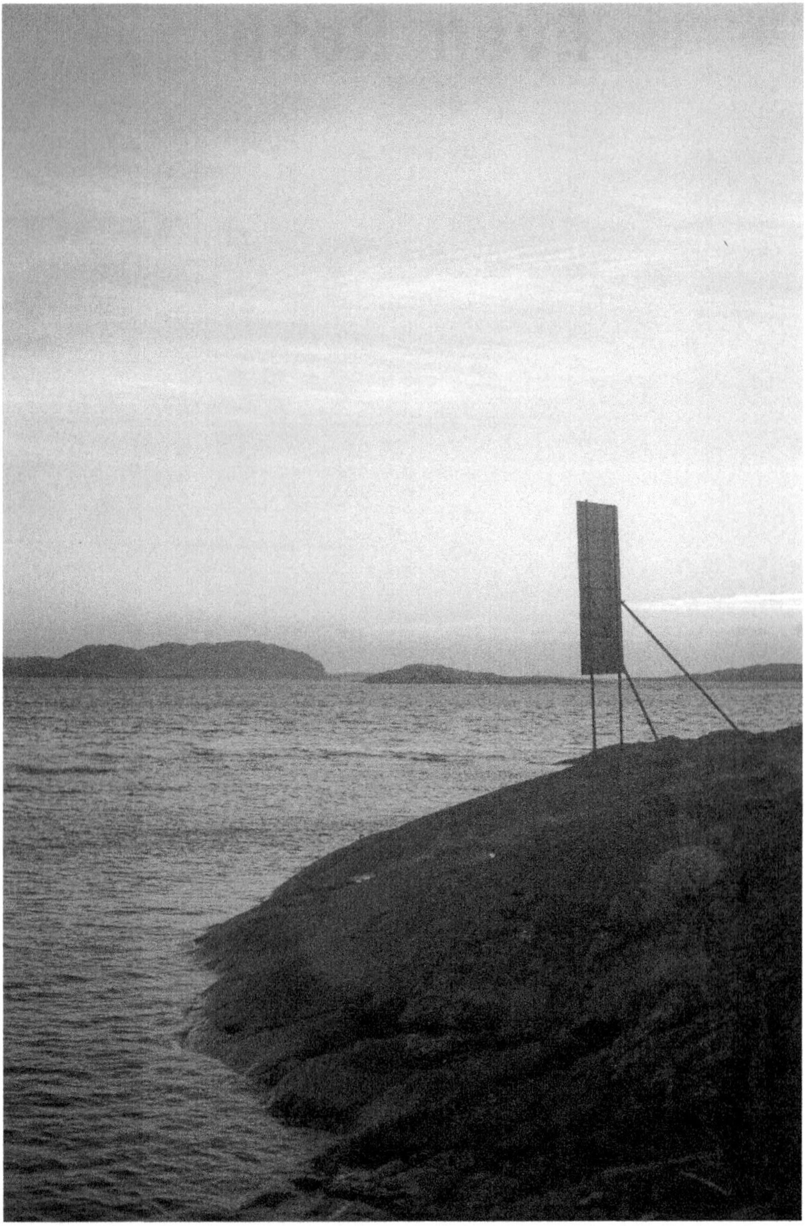

Evan Roth, *Internet Landscapes - Sweden,* 2016, Still, courtesy the artist.
Available online at http://n57.889503e11.685638.se/

For a long time, and for no particular reason, the Internet has been perceived mainly as a soul without a body: a dematerialized, invisible entity, filling the space between computers, allowing us to communicate almost instantly, and to travel from a website to another in the blink of an eye. The space of communication was virtual, while the physical world was the real world. Visiting the internet was described as "surfing." Together with the ocean, another seminal metaphorical reference was outer space: amateur websites were often sporting shiny starry night backgrounds, and both Netscape and Internet Explorer had references to space in their iconic logos. People who spent a lot of time online used the phrase "In Real Life" (IRL) to talk about what happened when they were offline. At the time, of course, the average Internet user knew, or could understand quite easily, that this "immaterial" network was made possible by the telephone physical infrastructure, which web pages were relying upon, and that emails were traveling through servers. They could even realize, if they thought about it for a minute, that home computers would end up very soon in a third world illegal dumpster, and that the cyberspace required a lot of electricity. Today, it's pretty different. We know that the Internet is real and what happens online is real. We changed too many devices to dismiss the fact that they may have an impact on the environment. We have been enslaved for too long to the endless flow of information to just enjoy it as surfing. We know that there are companies that are worth billions thanks to our data. We have seen pictures of data centers, maps of the undersea cable, construction sites with a sign saying that the fibre optic is coming soon. Despite all the rhetorics that accompanied the launch of wi-fi communication and cloud services, today our perception of the internet is less mystical and more secular and prosaic. We may still find David Bowie's description of the Internet as "an alien life form" [1] extremely sexy and fascinating, but today it's easier to understand it as a heavy, expensive, and pervasive man-made infrastructure.

And yet, this awareness is, again, a vague perception rather than an actual knowledge. We still travel through the electronic superhighway mostly in immaterial ways. The actual body of the Internet is yet to be explored. *Internet Landscapes*, by US born, Paris based artist Evan Roth, is a project that brings him to travel through the actual body of the Internet, by visiting and documenting some of its physical manifestations. More precisely, Roth is interested in visiting submarine fiber optic cable landing locations, places where a national or continental network gets connected to the global Internet, which allows people to communicate instantly with any part of the world. The artist selects these locations on a map and, whenever he has the chance to spend some time in a new country, and to fund his traveling, he visits them, doing audio and video recording.The results of this process are later turned into artworks. According to the artist, "visiting the Internet physically is an attempt to repair a relationship that has changed dramatically as the Internet becomes more centralized, monetized and a mechanism for global government spying. Through understanding and experiencing the Internet's physicality, one comes to understand the network not as a mythical cloud, but as a human made and controlled sy-

stem of wires and computers." [2]
The choice to visit submarine fiber optic cable landing locations is meaningful. Most of the Internet infrastructure is undersea and invisible to the human eye. Over the mainland, this gigantic, titanic body is turned into human scale. You may experience the vertigo of the data flow by visiting data centers and server farms, but there everything is recognizable and familiar. You see humans, technology, tangles of small colored cables, lights going on and off. You are probably close to a city. You are online. Submarine fiber optic cable landing locations are usually located in obscure places along a given country's shoreline. They are not meant to be visited, so they are hard to reach from the land. They are often far from the tourist's places. When you get there, you are alone with the cable, the ocean and the wind. It's so uneven to have visitors from the land that the signs informing about the presence of the cable are looking away from you, to the ships that may eventually get too close to the seaside. And yet there, the Internet is not everywhere, "all around you", but exactly where the sign is placed, and manifests itself physically. If you want to do a pilgrimage to the body of the Internet, they are the best places to visit, maybe the only place where you can be alone with the behemoth, spend time with it, meditate upon it.
The *Internet Landscapes* project is an actual journey. When you set out to do a journey, you can prepare your luggage, study maps, read travel guides, do vaccinations, prepare everything, but you are unlikely to know in advance what you'll experience, and what you'll find out. What Evan Roth found out when he

started visiting the "physical Internet" in the first place were simple landscapes, where the "Internet" layer is somehow removed. Interviewed, he said: "the longer I work on this new series, the more peripheral the Internet becomes in my thinking. I've been using the phrase "Internet landscapes" to informally describe the work, but lately I've been dropping the "Internet" and just calling them "landscapes" (which I think is more true to what they are)." And furthermore:

> "I wrestled quite a bit with how much evidence of the Internet to show in the frame. In the end, it was important to me that in this first piece of the series, there not be any cables or direct clues. As I move forward with the series, I will include footage of cables where it makes sense, but from the beginning I always had this vision in my mind of the lonely tree in an uncomfortable landscape." [3]

This is what he mostly pictured: lonely trees in uncomfortable landscapes. The map of the Internet became his own way to discover the world. The images and videos of the series can be simply enjoyed as such: landscape painting.

The Wanderer

Traveling to a remote location, in order to do landscape painting. The project *Internet Landscapes* sets itself in a long artistic tradition, that found its most complete realization in the Romantic myth of the wanderer. Today, traveling is mostly a finalized activity: we travel to a place, in order to do something. It happens very fast, and the journey has no value per se: it's just a means to an end, an in-between time frame. As a frequent flyer, Evan Roth knows this way of traveling very well, and probably the *Internet Landscapes* project started in the very same way: a series of trips to well researched locations, in order to experience the Internet physically. But while the project developed, the relationship between the act of travelling and its ends / destination slightly changed: the project became an opportunity to experience traveling in a different way, and this way affected the project and its final result. The Romantic wanderer is a heroic figure engaged in a never ending quest for the natural sublime. Although the sublime manifests itself better in some places than others, it can't be found in a specific location, and it isn't rooted into a specific feature or detail of a place. It's more about the overall atmosphere of a place, and it can be experienced through silence, solitude and immersion. Like in Caspar David Friedrich's *Wanderer Above the Sea of Fog* (1818), or in Gustave Courbet's *Le Bord de mer à Palavas* (1854), the wanderer is always alone in nature; and although clouds, waves, trees, mountains, rocks, ruins and religious symbols can be often found in romantic landscapes, the sublime does not manifest itself in these single elements, but in their combination, and in the visual language developed by the artist.

Looking for the Internet in submarine fiber optic cable landing locations, the wanderer Evan Roth realizes that the Internet can't be captured by simply shooting the cables, or by pointing the camera to the cable warning signs; and can't be portrayed via documentary means. These pictures, that he sometimes takes, can be good for Instagram, or for the lectures he sometimes gives about the project. Here, in these places where the Internet becomes an invisible yet perceivable part of the landscape, it can be captured only by spending time with it, and by developing a new (audio) visual language.

The visual language adopted for the project is infrared photography. Rarely used in visual arts, infrared photography is a conceptual reference to the architecture of the Internet, which is infrared laser light transmitted through fiber optic cables. Infrared cameras are widely used in the security industry, in such a way that their aesthetics are now intimately connected with our daily experience of pervasive surveillance. A less obvious, but very important, reference is to the practices of paranormal researchers, that informs the work done with the audio, too, as we will see below. As the artist explains, paranormal researchers

> "have developed their own technologies to help them visualize and communicate with an invisible world of disembodied human energy [...] Ghost hunting technologies, like many of today's social media platforms, are made by believers who attempt (and often fail) to use technology to give us human and emotional connections to people we rarely see in person. I find these tools inspirational and relevant in helping me reconnect with the Internet." [4]

As a ghost hunter, Evan Roth developed his own infrared camera by hacking an ordinary camera, which allowed him to adjust it to his aesthetic and conceptual needs (the camera is shooting near the 1550 nanometer range of the electromagnetic spectrum, which is a common modulation for infrared data transport through fiber optic).

Visually, infrared photography adds a layer of abstraction to the image or the video. It alters the image in such a way that ma-

kes us less sensitive to phenomenological aspects of the single landscape (the light of the day, the color of the sea, the beauty or ugliness of the details). These landscapes make us think more to the sinopy of a fresco, or to a white marble low relief, than to documentary photography. Infrared photography turns the image into something poetic, painterly, eternal, magic.
Something similar happens with the audio. Roth custom built an instrumental transcommunication device based on the spirit box, a tool commonly used in paranormal communities that scans radio frequencies at regular intervals, recording a mix of white noise and audio fragments. His version reads his own pulse and changes radio frequencies in real time with his heart rate. The final result is composed of a mix of ambient sounds from the surrounding nature, along with fragments of local radio frequencies controlled through the spirit box.
In other words, Evan Roth is using contemporary means of communication in order to capture, in the tradition of romantic landscape painting, the invisible (and inaudible) level of reality: the one at which the Internet manifests itself as an endless data flow.

Kites

The journey of the wanderer is always a travel through time, and within himself. By traveling, the wanderer often meditates on the traces left by human history on the landscape, and engages a visible transformation of his own mind. Romantic travel tales are always bildungsroman: think to John Bunyan's *The Pilgrim's Progress*, or Jonathan Swift's *Gulliver's Travels*, as famous examples. Engaging his quest for the traces of the physical Internet in space, Roth also engaged a pilgrimage through time: exploring the tradition of romantic painting, the history of the Internet and of communication technologies, and the intersections between the two. For example he discovered that Samuel Morse, the inventor of the Morse code, was also an amateur landscape painter.

On a personal level, Roth discovered his own difficulties about standing alone in nature. After years of compulsive web surfing, hyperactive tab jumping, multitasking and instant communication he, as probably most of us, initially found the experience of nature and loneliness extremely boring. As he explained:

> "When I'm in the field filming, I usually shoot still tripod shots between 10 and 15 minutes in duration. Because I'm recording audio (both from the ambient surroundings as well as from the radio spectrum), I need to remain stationary for the entire duration of the clip. In that sense the filming process is like a digital retreat with mandatory periods of 15 minutes of solitary meditation in nature. And what was most striking to me when I started this process was not "omg, this retreat into nature and being away from screens is amazing!", it was more, "holy shit, this is boring." In the beginning I found myself negotiating internally whether certain shots were worth the 15 minutes of stillness that was required. As I continued with the project, however, this perception of time became one of the most interesting aspects of the work." [5]

On a broader, more general level, the *Internet Landscapes* project is the consequence of his personal need to review his past approach to communication technologies, and the road that brought him to his current view. *Internet Landscapes* are his coming-of-age story. These two levels of traveling are what brought Roth to print his landscapes on kites, instead of making regular photo prints. As a children's game, kites work as a reference to Roth's juvenile, spontaneous approach to the Internet as a medium, and to his coming-of-age process. In the history of electronic communications, however, kites are one of the first tools used to experiment with transatlantic wireless communications. More specifically, in December 1901 Guglielmo Marconi successfully used six hexagonal kites to transmit radio waves over the ocean. Roth's kites reference Marconi's kites both in size and shape, while at the same time hinting to the hexagram shape often used to represent the Internet in patent filings.

Web Sites

While the *Internet Landscapes* pictures have been turned into kites, the audio and video recordings have been used to build websites. By visiting them, the viewer may be struck by the level of "site unspecificity" they seem to display. The URL is impossible to recall, and to type: you need a straight link, or to copy and paste it. Videos are embedded full page, but they are vertical and don't resize, so you always see just a part of the image. The soundtrack looks like white noise. According to the habits of current web surfing, you probably open them on a browser tab, among many others. Try to spend time with them, without checking your Facebook account every thirty seconds or so. It's hard. It's boring.

The best way to experience them is probably in an exhibition space, on a vertical screen. There, you can enjoy them as paintings. Roth tried out various solutions: setting up installations reminiscent of the "cable alert" signs he found on submarine fiber optic cable landing locations; or on wall, on huge flat screens or miniaturized on tiny LCD displays. In the exhibition space, we can enjoy them as a simple aesthetic experience: an exercise in immersion, contemplation and slowness. On a web browser, they are background noise at best. So, why are they online?

A website may look like a painting, but it's not a painting. Behind the surface, there are a lot of levels you can play with. There is a source code, that you can use to inform the browser about how to display the page, but also to hide information that is interesting only for human eyes. There are files that are assembled by the source code in order to turn an archive into a multimedia experience. These files are physically stored on a server located somewhere in the world, and are associated with a numerical address that can be translated into words. By typing this address, we activate a flow of information that travels from the server, through the cables, to our screen. Along this journey, information is converted into infrared light, and then again into information that is interpreted and displayed. By doing a website, instead of a painting, you can play with all these things, and Evan Roth does. For his websites, he bought server space in the countries he visited. Whenever we load them, we ask some data packets stored, for example, in Sweden, to travel through the very same place they represent to reappear on our computer. The web address - something like http://n57.630653e11.878293.se/ - is actually displaying the GPS coordinates of the place portrayed in the work: if we paste it in an online maps system such as Google Maps, we can experience a different way of "visiting" the place. But it may be even easier if we check the source code of the page. There we can find some useful information, including the Google Maps link of the visited location and a link to a traceroute information file, displaying the path of packets across an Internet Protocol (IP) network.

In other words, these websites are actually "web sites", places on the network that mirror both visually and conceptually the physical places they portray, in a complexity of layers and references that makes the experience of the project richer as long as we dig deep.

Text commissioned by Belenius/Nordenhake, Stockholm, and first published in the catalogue of the exhibition *Evan Roth – Kites & Websites*. Belenius/Nordenhake, Stockholm, and Aksioma, Institute for Contemporary Art, Ljubljana 2016 with the title "Internet Landscapes. A Journey in Space and Time". Online at http://aksioma.org/Kites-Websites-Evan-Roth.

[1] Check out David Bowie's 2000 BBC interview with Jeremy Paxman: www.factmag.com/2016/01/11/david-bowie-internet-jeremypaxman-interview/.

[2] Evan Roth, "Internet Landscapes. Project Outline", 2016, unpublished.

[3] Bani Brusadin, Ruth McCullough, Domenico Quaranta, "The more time I spend alone in nature, the more I forget about all of the politics surrounding the flow of data under my feet". Interview with Evan Roth, in Bani Brusadin, Eva and Franco Mattes, Domenico Quaranta (Eds.), *The Black Chamber. Surveillance, paranoia, invisibility & the internet*, exhibition catalogue, Link Editions and Aksioma, March 2016.

[4] Evan Roth, "Internet Landscapes. Project Outline", cit.

[5] B. Brusadin, R. McCullough, D. Quaranta, "The more time I spend alone in nature...", cit.

Addie Wagenknecht

2016

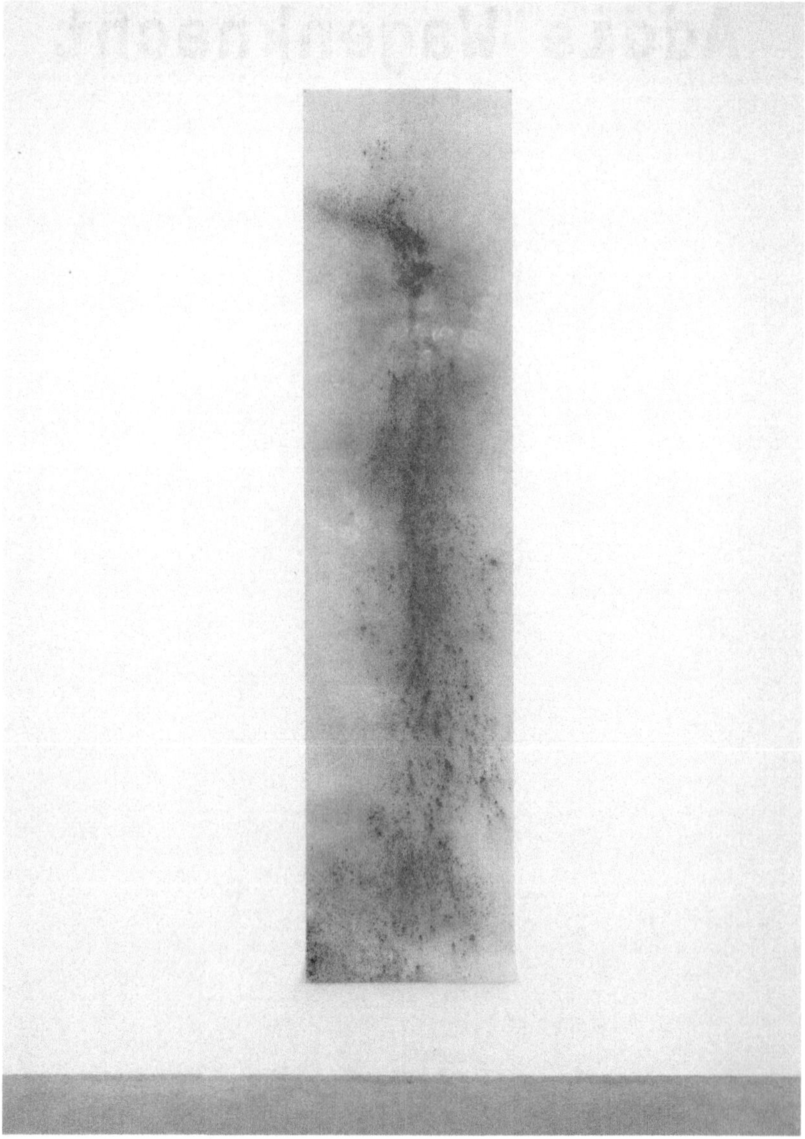

Addie Wagenknecht, *Agra at Dusk*, 2014. Gun powder, thermochromic pigment and beet-dyed pigment on vellum, 100 x 24 in / 254 x 61 cm. Courtesy Bitforms, New York.

1. *While You Were Sleeping* (2016) is a fifteen meters grey wingspan sculpture, shaped as a big military drone, apparently floating in the exhibition space thanks to a number of fiber optic cables that simultaneously hold it down to the floor and keep it suspended half a meter from it, in a kind of in-between state. The sculpture is intimidating and reassuring at the same time, somehow reminding of a huge wild beast that has been defeated and tied, yet is still alive, and ready to roar at us, her eyes full of hatred. Similarly, although the drone is silent and still, we can't be totally confident about the fact that it won't, at some point, start flying over us. A military drone doesn't show rage off, it's unmanned and impersonal; it's designed to fly unheard and unseen; but it can be remotely controlled, and sometimes it kills. The title itself is ambiguous and threatening: it may talk about a battle that took place overnight, when the vehicle was detected and captured; but it somehow also talks about what may happen every night, when aircrafts like this fly over our roofs, unseen.
Unmanned Aerial Vehicles, or UAVs, are a powerful visual metaphor of the relationship between technology and society. They are the output of military technological research, and they have been used in most wars from the Fifties onward, but they entered the public debate, and started inhabiting the collective imagination, only in recent years. As any war technology, they have been allegedly developed to make the war shorter, cleaner, more effective, and less dangerous in terms of human losses; but actually, they have made it more inhuman, frightening and ubiquitous. They could be used for a

number of civil and recreational purposes, and as any technology, they can be hacked and turned for the good; but in reality, they are mostly adopted in military operations for missions that are too "dull, dirty or dangerous" [1] for manned aircraft; and out of that, they are widely used for policing and surveillance.

To reference Dr. Melvin Kranzberg's first law of technology, "Technology is neither good nor bad; nor is it neutral." [2] Addie Wagenknecht's grey wingspan drone effectively visualizes this lack of neutrality. It's harmless, but it scares us anyway; it reminds us that we are constantly watched, and of the many drone missions in which people died without even seeing their enemy, and without even knowing that they were under attack. To paraphrase Kranzberg, this technology's interaction with our social ecology had consequences that went far beyond its immediate purposes: made to make us feel more safe, the ultimate weapon of the war on terror spawned more terror and more terrorists, and made us feel more insecure and paranoid.

While You Were Sleeping is part of a series of sculptural works in which Addie Wagenknecht depicts an unsettling scenario, in which surveillance, paranoia, data abundance and violence seem to prevail. Exemplary of this approach is *Asymmetric Love* (2013), a piece in which seven CCTV cameras and a number of DSL internet cables are assembled in order to mimic an iconic baroque chandelier. Hanged to the ceiling as a true chandelier, the piece dissimulates surveillance by hiding it into a familiar object with a familiar function; but when one actually sees it, it becomes even more threatening than a single, functional camera: nothing seems able to escape this seven-eyed hydra, that's reminiscent of the nine-eyed camera of the Google Street View car. The shape of the chandelier has been also used by Wagenknecht in *Liberator Rounds* (2015), in which she mounted on a custom metal body eleven 3D printed replicas of the "Liberator", the first 3D modeled open source handgun made available for download online. The digital model of the Liberator was later used to shape the *Liberator Vases* (2016), a work done in collaboration with Martin Zangerl and Stefan Hechenberger. In these works, the model is deformed, clustered and turned useless, in a way that points to the subversive power of appropriation and creativity but also to the fact that a gun is a gun. And like Checkov's gun, if it's in the story, it should be fired.

A sense of awe and threat also permeates *Data and Dragons* (2013 - 2014), a series of custom printed circuit boards that intercept and log data from their surrounding. The black circuit boards, with their green flashing lights and their black ethernet cables, bring the server aesthetics to the exhibition space. Like silent, pacific monsters, they ingest and digest our data; and although these data are never shared with anything or anybody, but just processed by the machines and kept completely anonymous, they also reveal how pervasive and seamless surveillance can be.

Surveillance is a major concern in all Wagenknecht's recent work. Surveillance is not just that of the CCTV cameras installed everywhere, or of the drone flying over our roofs; it's also that of data captured along their way over the network. As she said in an interview: ""The question for me is how does non-scarce data tie into surveillance? If data is ubiquitous, so is surveillance." [3] These data are intercepted, stolen, recorded by companies and institutions, but are, in most of the cases, willingly shared by us, who have been seduced and imprisoned by a system in which we apparently enjoy being watched by other people. Writing about Bentham's panopticon, Michel Foucault notes:

> "Hence the major effect of the Panopticon: to induce in the inmate a state of conscious and permanent visibility that assures the automatic functioning of power. So to arrange things that the surveillance is permanent in its effects, even if it is discontinuous in its action; that the perfection of power should tend to render its actual exercise unnecessary; that this architectural apparatus should be a machine for creating and sustaining a power relation independent of the person who exercises it; in short, that the inmates should be caught up in a power situation of which they are themselves the bearers." [4]

In the current panopticon, we expect to be watched also when we aren't - to such an extent that we may be even disappointed when we discover that we aren't. Surveillance can be sexy, as in *Love Lies* (2014), an installation made of cameras adorned with fake swarovski crystals; but it's often invisible, although expected, and turning it visible and physical is one of the motivations behind these works.

2. In fact, what Wagenknecht is doing is not just portraying in dark tints the present time - it's also an attempt to actively change the future. As she wrote:

> "We're not descending into chaos, but into complexity. The Internet connects everything around us, and we're uncovering infinite amounts of complexity by examining its infrastructure and rules as they are leaked, thanks to people like Snowden and Manning. We're also finding ways to subvert and change how things are versioned or controlled." [5]

Although Wagenknecht recognizes that the utopian moment of the internet is over, she still has a strong belief in the subversive potential of hacking, in the transformative power of art and education, and in the need to be engaged and oppositional. An open source programmer and an open hardware developer, she still recognizes the strong influence that activist groups like Guerrilla Girls had in her choice to embrace art practice. She believes that "systems create control and at the same time create methods of how that control can be defied and subverted. Tools can be used to make things as much as they can be used to break things down", [6] as by forcing a drone to paint or making some roomba vacuum cleaning machines go mad and destroy each other (*Internet of Things*, 2016). She said about her work:

> "A lot of contemporary art is boring and too easy. My whole approach in analysing the world is very different. Is it oppositional? Yes. Is it intentionally oppositional? Yes. I want to change the system, not make it more pretty to look at. There is a responsibility to focus, dream, ask questions, and burn up the things that culture doesn't need to make space for what we do." [7]

One way to change the system may be to set up an all female hacker and art collective, as Wagenknecht did by founding, back in 2014, Deep Lab. Deep Lab is one way among others to fight against the glass ceiling, an expression describing the invisible barriers through which women can see elite positions but are kept away from them. Through education, according to Wagenknecht, woman can become dangerous, and so more powerful. [8] *Glass Ceiling* is also the title of a series of performances, in which the artist fights against some large bullet proof glasses in different attempts to break them: by kissing them with lipstick (thus using her femininity as a weapon), by throwing donuts or cakes against them (criticism), or by actually attempting to break them with rocks, injuring herself in the while. All these attempts end up in a failure, but being successful in the short term is not the point; what's important is to keep fighting.

The lack of reference, in this and other works, to the online strengthening, rather than weakening, the consistency of Wagenknecht's work, which is not about the network, but about society: a society that is, however, more and more "becoming a byproduct of the network." [9]

Text commissioned by MU, Eindhoven and HeK, Basel and first published in the catalogue of the exhibition *Liminal Laws - Addie Wagenknecht*, MU and HeK, 2016 with the title "Descending Into Complexity". The book is available at www.mu.nl/nl/shop/liminal-laws.

[1] Brian P. Tice, "Unmanned Aerial Vehicles – The Force Multiplier of the 1990s", in *Airpower Journal*, Spring 1991, referenced in *Wikipedia*, https://en.wikipedia.org/wiki/Unmanned_aerial_vehicle .

[2] Melvin Kranzberg, "Technology and History: "Kranzberg's Laws"", in *Technology and Culture*, Vol. 27, No. 3 (Jul., 1986), pp. 544-560.

[3] Jordan Pearson, "Sex Cams and Voyeurism Make for Great Art", in *Motherboard*, August 8, 2014, online at http://motherboard.vice.com/read/sex-cams-and-voyeurism-make-for-great-art.

[4] Michel Foucault, "Panopticism", in *Discipline & Punish: The Birth of the Prison*, New York, Vintage Books 1995, pp. 195-228.

[5] David Riley, "Deep Lab. CHAOS TO COMPLEXITY", in *Topical Cream*, March 2, 2015, online at http://topicalcream.info/editorial/deep-lab-2.

[6] Personal communication, April 2016.

[7] Rosa Abbott, "Baby I Got Your Money: Addie Wagenknecht Interview", in *Totally Dublin*, 2014. Online at http://totallydublin.ie/arts-culture/arts-culture-features/baby-got-money-addie-wagenknecht-interview/.

[8] David Riley, "Deep Lab. CHAOS TO COMPLEXITY", cit.

[9] Mike Pepi, "Suppression Architectures: An Interview with Addie Wagenknecht", in *Art in America*, December 3, 2014, online at www.artinamericamagazine.com/news-features/interviews/suppression-architectures-an-interview-with-addie-wagenknecht/.

Made in the USA
Middletown, DE
10 March 2022

62440112R00106